GLIMPSES OF A POST-CAPITALIST FUTURE

GLIMPSES OF A POST-CAPITALIST FUTURE

ADAM COWART

CRAIG PERRY

MONICA PORTEANU

POLINA SILAKOVA

STEPHEN AGUILAR-MILLAN (Editor)

DESIGN BY ACCIDENT PRESS 2019

First published 2019 by the Design By Accident Press, a division of Design By Accident Limited.

ISBN: 9781686731495

Design By Accident Press
The Greenways Partnership
25 St Margaret's Green
Ipswich
IP4 2BN
United Kingdom

www.eufo.org

GLIMPSES OF A POST-CAPITALIST FUTURE

Table of Contents

Introduction

How did we get here?

The European Futures Observatory (EUFO to its friends) was established in 2004 with three purposes. First, to provide a vehicle through which the practice of futures could be demonstrated to a wider public. Second, to provide a vehicle through which young futurists could gain practical experience to enhance their CVs. Third, to help to develop a European approach to the study of the future.

In order to achieve these objectives, we developed a programme of Internships. These ran from 2004 to 2016. Each programme ran for one year. We worked in conjunction with the World Future Society to deliver the programme, with a deliverable of presenting a paper of our findings at the annual WFS conference and having published as a book chapter the outcomes of our studies.

This worked very well. It gave us a chance to present to a wider audience some of the practice of the study of the future. It gave the participants a real project to add to their CVs. An important principle of our work within EUFO is that it all must be capable of being placed in the public domain. This means that the participants can easily reference their contribution to a project, and that project can be presented to a wider audience as an example of what futurists do. It also allowed us to give greater focus on a more European approach to the study of the future.

In developing this European approach, it might help to explain how this fits into the constellation of futures. Much of the future work emanating from North America tends to be technology heavy. If there were to be a North American approach to the study of the future, it would be described in terms of advancing technologies and how they may shape the future. Alternatively, much of the work about the future emanating from Asia tends to be values driven. The studies could be defined in terms of mapping human values and how they may change in the coming years. As a juxtaposition, a European approach would emphasise a more societal and institutional aspect dimension to the study of the future. It would describe how the interaction of people, both individually and collectively, would act to shape the future.

Of course, these caricatures are gross exaggerations with numerous exceptions that prove the caricature wrong. However, as an approach to the future, it has dominated our work. The pieces in this volume are people centred, they are light on technology, and they only make reference to values where they are needed.

The World Future Society changed ownership in 2016 and embarked on a new strategic direction. This left our Interns programme without a natural home. In a parallel development, the Association of Professional Futurists (APF) had run an Emerging Fellows programme over 2014-15. It was organised much along the lines of the EUFO Interns programme, but with a deliverable of a monthly blog post from the members of the programme.

In 2017, discussions began about the possibility of EUFO taking responsibility for the running of the APF Emerging Fellows programme as part of a joint venture. These discussions bore fruit, Emerging Fellows were recruited, and the revived Emerging Fellows programme was launched at the start of 2018.

What did we hope to achieve?

At the outset, the objective of the revived programme was to generate a body of futures content that the APF could publish in its blog, to provide the participants with an experience of curated writing for a year, and to generate sufficient content for EUFO to publish in book form.

Our first task was to recruit a body of Emerging Fellows for the programme. The 2018 participants were recruited mainly from the APF membership. We allowed a relatively free rein in the object of their enquiry, although we did insist upon the delivery of twelve pieces in order to complete the programme successfully.

This turned out to be a mixed bag. On the one hand, it meant that we could get away to a good start. On the other hand, it also meant that the participants came from a rather narrow range of experience. In future programmes, we may try to cast the net more widely for participants, to incorporate views of the future that may not necessarily be captured through APF membership.

The Emerging Fellows would provide the content of a blog post of 500 to 700 words each month from each participant for the APF. Although we allowed a free rein in terms of the topics considered, we felt that a general theme ought to be in terms of a number of glimpses of what a post-capitalist future might be. We had no definite views about the time horizon, so the pieces are vague as to exactly when these glimpses might be seen.

In retrospect, we perhaps ought to have been a little more focussed in terms of content. There were times when the narrative could drift a little and we all could have benefitted from a more distinct focus. Future programmes are likely to be more to the point, with a clearer structure and more clearly defined goals. We are also likely to give greater emphasis at the outset of the commitment needed to complete the programme successfully. The 2018 programme had a dropout rate that we considered rather high.

We frowned upon the academic style of writing. One of the objects of the programme was to help the participants develop a style and voice that they will need in practice. Short sentences. Simple words. Accessible English. This proved to be a bit of a challenge to some participants but those who completed the programme have shown an improvement in their writing. We have managed to curate an eclectic set of writings which we present to a wider audience.

What have we achieved?

It is time to introduce the work of the Emerging Fellows who successfully completed the programme. Each has brought their own distinct style to their writing and each has brought their own distinct approach to the problem which they set themselves.

Adam Cowart set himself the task of answering the question: To what extent will the real economy be real in the future? This is a fascinating question set in a world of a de-materialised economy and with weightless companies. Much of the modern economy is intangible and Adam set himself the task of examining how far this process could go. For those involved in the future of business, the future of work, or the future of consumer behaviour, this piece raises some interesting questions. It also provides some interesting answers.

Craig Perry set himself the task of answering the question: Is another great power war inevitable? As the United States and China drift towards increasing tension and conflict, some have argued that war between the two is inevitable. But is it? Craig examines this question from a number of dimensions before concluding that probably we can all sleep easy. For now.

Monica Porteanu set herself the ask of examining decision making for the regenerative society. It seems that we live currently in a deeply polarised society. The question is how society might heal itself? What processes are there that will enhance this process? Monica explores the mechanisms by which the healing process could begin and examines what some of the pre-conditions for this might be.

Polina Silakova set herself the question: Would a post-capitalist economy be one which catered for values more than possessions? In answering this question, Polina gets to the heart of examining exactly where value lies in our transactions. She then goes on to consider how that may change as we move into the future, before coming to a distinct view on where future value resides.

Each of these pieces is commendable in themselves. As a body of work, they provide an interesting view on a disparate range of potential futures. They all have common elements – digitisation, AI, the experience economy – but their value lies in their differences. In resolving these differences, we can learn something about our emergent future.

Stephen Aguilar-Millan

To What Extent Will The Real Economy Be Real In The Future?

1. When Money Grows Wings and Flies Away

2. Get Real

3. A Virtual Reality Museum Tour in 2030

4. The Future of Paracosm Economies

5. The End of a (Virtual) Way of Life

6. Welcome to Earth, the Sub Optimized Planet

7. Superposition and Frosting a Cake

8. Ugh, Scenarios? That's Not Very Innovative...

9. Transitioning to a New Form of Innovation

10. The Make Believe Economy

11. The World is turning into a Pumpkin Patch

12. Fake It Till You Make It

When Money Grows Wings and Flies Away

On March 19, 2014, in a Canadian courtroom, 66-year-old Arlan Galbraith was convicted of fraud of over $5,000 and sentenced to a little over seven years in jail. While all agree that he lost millions of dollars of other people's money ($42 million to be precise, and contractual obligations to pay another $356 million), many, including some of his victims, are still unsure of whether he wilfully defrauded them.

In 2001, Arlan founded Pigeon King Industries. The concept was simple. Pigeon King would sell you a set of breeding pigeons for a certain cost, and agree to buy back all offspring at a fixed rate over the next 10 years. Over time the story of what the business model would be, exactly, shifted. First, the pigeons would be sold to the supposedly lucrative pigeon racing industry, then the story changed to a plan to sell squab meat. In actuality, the offspring were sold to other farmers as breeding pairs, and the excess pigeons were housed at Pigeon Kings' expense. Ostensibly the plan involved a period of building a "network of breeders" before taking over the world. Eventually, farmers and government got leery. Pigeon inventory started to rise as Pigeon King continued to honour contractual agreements, buying up offspring, despite a dwindling number of buyers. Barns were retrofitted to house the excess inventory. Funds were spent to feed and vaccinate the exploding population. Finally, farmers willing to sign on dried up. Without new buyers, Pigeon King couldn't pay their existing breeders and the whole thing fell apart.

Sound familiar? Kind of like a Ponzi scheme except, instead of money, the currency was pigeons?

How real will the real economy be in the future? We shall explore how fiction turns to reality, reality turns into fiction, and how this will shape the future of the real economy. Reality and fiction are often at war with each other. Perhaps we inherently move between periods in which reality is dominant and periods where fiction/myth dominate. In our most recent fictional turn away from the real, we now have the destructive tools and technologies (and some very good reasons to escape from reality) that allow us to bore deeper and deeper into the mystical archetypal hearts of our own dreams and collective desires. And with this deepening of unreality, we take our systems and structures with us: families, politics and, yes, the economy.

What is the financial market if not a future bet on a compelling story? Between the virtual and financial economies, how will the real economy be influenced? Will it become a "puppet" economy for its two bigger and stronger cousins? Or, with scarcity and limits to growth, will it come roaring back as the dominant economic sphere? Since we abandoned the gold standard, have we drifted into a hyper-real economy from which there is no escape? If late-capitalism requires constant new areas of growth to survive, does the turn to a fictional economy create limitless new areas of expansion?

As for our poor unwanted pigeons, after health and city officials warned of a potential release of the birds, and with the spectre of a mass migration to Toronto, where they would blacken the skies and overwhelm parks, much like their now extinct Carrier cousins, the birds were slaughtered en masse. Drowned. Gassed. Burned. Hundreds of millions of fictional dollars. Up in smoke.

Sounds familiar, doesn't it?

Get Real

Our current economic system, and all the social and political systems tied to it, requires perpetual growth.

Growth not only underpins the financial economy, but the real economy as well, which requires new goods and services (or more demand for the same) to expand. The end of growth would mean the collapse of financial markets and stagnation in the real economy. It would also lead to social and political upheaval due to financial inequality. The socio-political perspective that underlies our obsession with growth is the presumption that lower and middle class citizens will accept massive inequality as long as their lives (and wages) get incrementally better, year after year. We would all love to have that private yacht, but are content as long as our annual salary increase allows us to take that Alaskan cruise. And this incremental improvement does not come from increased economic equality or financial redistribution; it is a result of growth.

Another long standing economic assumption is that, as jobs are automated, new forms of work will emerge. While some estimates follow a historically consistent trend of 10% job displacement in the foreseeable future, other estimates predict an acceleration of displacement, up to 50%. If job displacement does enter the 50% range, the creation of as-yet-unknown jobs, at such significantly high numbers in a relatively short period of time, seems unlikely. Even minor displacement can have a significant disruptive effect on political and social cohesion. But there is another option for continual growth in the real economy: instead of creating new jobs, simply commoditize things that people are currently doing for free.

Paul Mason alludes to this in his book "Post-Capitalism" when he suggests that in order to make this a scalable economic area of growth, we "would require the mass commercialization of ordinary human life." Late capitalism appears to be stealing a few plays from the feminist economics playbook. While media attention has largely been focused on pay equity between genders, some of the foundational work in feminist economics has focused on care work and intra-household bargaining. It is not much of a stretch to interpret Mason's "ordinary human life" as the traditional perspective of unpaid "women's work".

If one is looking for a macro-trend in the real economy, one need look no further than the colonization of social interaction by the economy. This is evident in the more ubiquitous forms of social media, but is also increasingly prevalent in more innocuous forms. Consider the cuddle party, a social media coordinated interaction where strangers come together out of a desire to cuddle (and watch a movie). Organizations such as "Nurse Next Door" look after the elderly, Christmas dinner can be ordered online, and chore apps convince kids to (continue) to do work around the house "for free". The company "Do My Stuff" has succinctly defined the overall trend with their slogan "Outsource your life".

Anyone considering a new business could start with the question "What are people doing today for free, that I can get them to pay for tomorrow?" Of course the question now must be asked, if every tiny component of our existence becomes commoditized and outsourced, are we even real anymore?

Virtual Reality Museum Tour in 2030: "To Your Left, We Have a Stuffed Dodo Bird; To Your Right, A Stuffed Entrepreneur"

Ah, the entrepreneur. Nothing is more real, more visceral. 100 years ago, the image of the entrepreneur was a man with greased back hair, an impressive handlebar moustache, a three-piece suit, standing solemnly beside some heavy piece of blackened machinery. Fast-forward to the 90's, and it was young, awkward white boys, doing their best to look cool but not quite pulling it off. And now today, a moderately more diversified group of men and women, usually not quite facing the camera, more turned to the side, as if the camera has just caught them in the act of doing something extraordinarily innovative, something just outside the frame. What's consistent across all these images is a certain twinkle in the eye, as if communicating to the viewer across time and space, "Hey, I can see the future. Can you?"

To sustain a real economy requires not only the ongoing production and consumption of existing products, but the creation of new products. These new products are developed and produced by large and medium sized companies, along with small and new businesses. Entrepreneurs are considered critical for a healthy and dynamic economy. They provide an infusion of new ideas, disrupt old business models, and create new areas of growth and opportunity.

But are entrepreneurs going the way of the Dodo? While much has been written on how entrepreneurs and big business are, and will, use AI to change the world and the economy, less has been written on how AI will disrupt the disruptors. New business and product ideas are, after all, essentially the output of synthesizing insights, developing and testing prototypes, procuring capital for production and expansion, and then running the business. When will we start seeing entrepreneur bots? Autonomous product and service creation programs who generate business ideas and then go out and make the business a reality?

Consider how advanced programs have disrupted market trading, in particular the well-known story of high frequency trading. Minute market fluctuations are exploited by advanced algorithms. Take this same rapid response approach to the real economy and AI bots. These bots could be perpetually scouring global markets for tiny opportunities, and move rapidly to capitalize on those blips in the market to make a profit before the blip disappears and the markets return to "normal". Along with online sales, the concept of the "pop up shop" could become incredibly ubiquitous. An AI Entrepreneur identifies a local opportunity in, say, Winnipeg Canada. A generic pop up store is procured, product is developed, rapidly prototyped, market tested in minutes by customer-composite bots, specs sent to other, manufacturing bots, the product is created and on the shelf (and available online) within a day. Within a week, the opportunity has been exploited, and the store closes down. Perhaps inventory lingers online for a brief period of time.

We have been considering whether the real economy will, in fact, be real in the future. A vertically integrated AI product and service creation network could function largely independently of humans. With the capability to generate and produce new products and services far faster than humans can possibly consume them, does this follow the conceptual trend of hypercapitalism? Will the speed and intensity of economic activity continue to accelerate? Forget about getting irritated by a new iPhone every year – with our entrepreneur and product-creation bots, we could have a new iPhone once a week. Perhaps even once a day.

Of course, the next logical step for humans, overwhelmed by choice and upgrades, is for us to outsource our consumer decision making to our own bots. B2B (Business to Business) models will gradually shift towards an AIB2B model, and then eventually to an AIB2AIB model (Artificial Intelligence Business to Artificial Intelligence Business). While most sci-fi movies imagine a dystopian future of nuclear wars caused by a "woke" robot, would the invasion be far less innocuous? Whoever controls the economy controls everything. But is this economy still real?

The Future of Paracosm Economies

We've been exploring just how real the real economy will be in the future. Not just the inherent "realness" of the economy, but the relevance of the real. Will the real economy continue to exist in any meaningful way in the future? The answer, at least in this particular case, is an emphatic "No!"

Paracosm refers to an imaginary world, usually a very elaborate imaginary world, developed by a child early in their life. It may or may not stay with them into adulthood. Psychiatrists have used the term to denote a process of understanding loss and tragedy in early childhood by retreating into the imagination. The historical image of this is well known: A Victorian-era child sits despondent in a garden somewhere, the only adult who ever really loved them now dead; they are wearing formal "adult" clothes that in no way are conducive for garden-exploring; they are pale, forlorn, at the mercy of a world devoid of happiness. Their only escape will be an active imagination, a world of characters and high drama, a world just barely in their control.

Indeed, most early examples of paracosms and their creators (paracosmists) are the usual crowd: Emily Bronte and her paracosm "Gondal", J.R.R. Tolkien and the languages of middle-earth (the imaginary characters would emerge sometime after the imaginary languages that they spoke), Henry Darger, the "outsider" artist, who invented the world of the Vivian Sisters in his teens, and many others. Paracosms are considered a sign of high intelligence in children, an example of "worldplay".

Beyond the rather obvious economic value of the imagination in contributing to books, film and art in the physical world, what do paracosms have to do with the economy? The answer is in how we reconceive of that image of the precocious child. They are no longer wearing frilly Victorian garments, spending hours alone in a vast garden finding respite from disapproving servants. They have taken their imaginations online, and are increasingly being given the tools to construct their imaginative worlds – not out of words, not out of inanimate toys, or the rocks and sticks lying about the garden. But in the virtual world.

Consider a few ongoing trends. Prosumerism, where we generate our own products. The end of growth which, presumably, means children yet to be born will not enjoy the abundance that we currently fail to fully appreciate. And, of course, the multi-streamed and nefarious ways in which companies are trying to tap into (and latch onto) the hearts, minds, and imaginations of children at the earliest age possible.

In the future, a nearly infinite area of growth will be our imaginations. We often look at "developing" nations as under-exploited areas of opportunity. Meanwhile, every child is walking around with a world of undercapitalized voices in their heads that could become its own nation, its own economy.

Imagine the two warring moons in a distant galaxy, and the market potential for their military industrial complex. Imagine a happily married couple, she a talking car, he a unicorn, navigating the exciting but expensive world of reproductive medicine to help them start a family of their own. The paradigm shift at play is moving from the current virtual market, which relies on human exchange on behalf of their avatars, to a virtual world of virtual exchange between multiple avatars created by a single human. Likely with no human knowledge of the exchange.

What does the rise and fall of our civilizations look like? Will they continue to exist after we are gone (regardless of their future growth potential)? A soulless universe without a creator that exists only for the pursuit of profit? Or will they be tied to us as if by a virtual umbilical cord?

The End of a (Virtual) Way of Life

10,000 years ago, our economies were largely mobile and borderless. We roamed, we hunted, we foraged. One of the earliest clashes of economic models was when land ownership and borders, spurred on by the Agricultural Revolution, disrupted the nomadic lives of a decreasing proportion of the population. From the earliest evolutionary days of humanity until now, hunting and gathering was the dominant societal and economic model for approximately 90% of our history. Today, nomadic peoples number around 40 million.

Parallels between nomadic hunter-gatherer societies and contemporary, Generation X knowledge workers were made in the late 90's. But these observations were more often than not quirky, meant to emphasize a "new" way of working. Not to mention participate in a bit of generational bashing that has not evolved a whole lot now that it is being applied to millennials.

Foraging societies are typically characterized as not placing value on fixed resources (i.e. land). They are collective, typically non-hierarchical, societies with immediate-return economies. They derive benefits from their activities immediately, not in a delayed-return economy where benefits from activities occur over a period of time and are often associated with property rights of some sort.

Virtual foraging is such an innate activity that we do not even consider it as such – no different than our nomadic ancestors. We "search" the web for what we are looking for, we hunt, and we roam across countries and worlds. While traditionally this has meant searching for food, what real difference is there between finding food, and finding information that can be utilized in such a way as to monetize that information and purchase food? Virtual foraging and knowledge work is not typically an immediate-return economic environment, but the other characteristics of a foraging society are evident in the form of non-hierarchical groups without fixed resources, exploring open spaces.

Much has been written about censorship and net neutrality. There is still a very strong assumption that the virtual world is an open, borderless world. But as we increasingly migrate, and colonize virtual spaces, will this continue? The bulk of the conversation has been at the micro level. We typically point to Big Brother-type influencers. Nefarious government organizations monitoring and censoring us, or corporations manipulating us. The issue is never us – it's someone else. At the macro level we see echoes of our old ways of living and working. Vast open plains, forests and oceans. A limitless world for us to wander and forage within. And the relatively brisk pace at which we have begun to colonize, divide, and weaponize this space.

We have an unnerving ability to replicate our collective behaviours across time and space. It took thousands of years to erect barriers and borders on earth, and less than 20 years to begin the process in the virtual world. This is our capitalist model in its truest form: find or create space, break it up into pieces, monetize those pieces, move on.

What else is left? Creating or finding more space. Making the intangible tangible. Taking the unreal and making it real. If it is unmonetized, monetize it. When the first group of settlers head for Mars, it should not surprise anyone if one of those settlers has already incorporated a new business. "Martian Fencing Ltd." You know, just in case.

Welcome to Earth, the Sub Optimized Planet

What role can - or will - innovation play in the future of the real economy? To begin, let's start with the simplest definition of innovation. Innovation is "creating results by doing new things." The "doing new things" part is fairly self-explanatory on the surface. It is the process of doing something in a way in which it was not done previously. Although, often, we may have done something, then stopped doing it, then started doing it again either aware or unaware of having done it in the past. But the "creating results" piece of the definition is less clear. What, precisely, is a result? A positive outcome? And, if so, a positive outcome for whom? We can say that, today, an innovative result is one in which we either save money, make money, or provide some sort of social or environmental good. But are those the results we should be aiming for? Do we care, or even understand, how these results impact and influence other components of the global system? And, for our purposes here, how will our definition of "results" evolve in the future? The point here is not to focus on types of results reporting, such as triple line or happiness index-type measurements. The purpose here is on the deeper structural challenges to "real" innovation.

There is no question that what we might call "innovation-offset" occurs across a system or multiple subsystems. How often does an innovation in one area generate an offsetting process inefficiency or product redundancy in another? Put another way, if you innovate in one area, to the detriment of another area, are you really innovating at all? And how would you even know?

Two common terms used to describe this phenomenon are sub optimization and shifting the burden. Sub optimization commonly refers to silo-type thinking within an organization. This leads to non-value added activities, redundancy, or diminished returns. Shifting the burden, on the other hand, is a term generally meant to describe a tendency to focus on resolving surface-level, symptomatic issues, pushing costs and negative externalities onto others.

What we might call "sub optimization ecosystems" are now a vital part of the real economy, not only the maintenance of them, but the perpetual attempts to circumnavigate them. By focusing on the self-interest of the firm at the expense of the larger system, we are inherently sub optimizing. We ostensibly innovate within a department, across a division, across a firm, across an industry, across multiple industries, then across whole economies. There is no escape.

Our attention has been focused on what we can call the migratory patterns of money. How it's shapes and structures tend to manifest. And here, we see a profitable innovation ecosystem, where activity and expenditure is its own reward. But wait, isn't innovation inherently messy? An iterative process of trial and error. "Fail fast to succeed sooner"?

Consider what percentage of global GDP is dedicated to activities that solve problems by creating new problems elsewhere. Cycles of pointless zero-sum innovation. At a time of complexity, instead of adopting the tools of social innovation and systems change, we have doubled down on the mercurial dark arts of sub optimization, masked as real innovation.

Superposition and Frosting a Cake

We previously challenged what is truly innovative versus sub optimization in some shape or form. We can now delve deeper into assumptions about innovation today. If we start with standpoint theory and situated knowledge, we can drill down a little deeper to reach the concept of situated imagination.

Situated imagination contends that knowledge is dependent upon our location: physically, economically, and socially, among other situating coordinates. Thus, imagination is an amalgamation, an alchemy of self and collective conditions, which influences not only meaning but the concept of the "not-yet real", in the words of Jean Paul Sartre.

In order to "do different things" we must be able to "think differently". Therefore, moving beyond sub optimization first requires an acknowledgement of what we could call "Situated Innovation". Situational innovation, the phenomenon of innovation being inherently connected to a particular observer or group of observers, is perhaps the most significant hidden cost in the global economy. Exercises in empathy can help to re-situate the observer, but typically this is done in a manner that is inherently sub optimizing.

While our discussion has largely revolved around the issue of space (across silos, organizations, and countries), time is another dimension in which we sub optimize. The most obvious example of this is shifting the burden of climate change onto future generations. But the issue also manifests in, for example, inter-generational organizational issues. Consider the sub optimization of the past. While not as obvious as the impact on the future, consider the many cost-benefits and projects built around past projections of the future, now the present. By sub optimizing within the present, we underutilize the past, which can have ripple effects into the future. Decisions are forgotten, goals are lost and abandoned. For every idea that survives, countless others falter at some point. A Darwinian perspective on ideas and past innovations is nothing more than permission to hold a bias towards old ideas.

Finally, beyond the space and time, is matter. Agential realism, and spacetimemattering, a theory developed by Karen Barad, provides another perspective on matter and meaning in innovation activities. Agential realism, at its core, is about the inherent entanglement of all things. Any act of observation creates the "agential cut" in which we include some things, and exclude a number of other possibilities. This temporary "cut" allows us to view a chunk of a thing, matter, in isolation, in order to gain a greater understanding of the thing we wish to observe. Hence, our observations of the world are inherently performative. Here, too, we see the challenge of innovation and the limits to our innovative capacities. Observationally, we must isolate an object as either a thing or process. By doing this, we ignore its connected (here, entangled) state of being.

Think of it like this: You are making a cake. Typically, you would wait until it cooled and then frost the whole cake. However, once this particular cake has cooled, you can no longer observe the cake as a whole. You see a piece of the cake and cut out that piece, cover it in frosting, and return the piece to the cake. Then you go about trying to find other pieces of the cake. Unable to see the whole cake at once, you are left with cutting, frosting, returning. In all likelihood, you will only frost a small portion of the cake. Even if you somehow manage to cut off and frost every piece of the cake, it will look more than a little strange! Later that evening, most guests at the party, blessed with the ability to observe the whole cake at once, will agree this is a far from optimum cake. Rather, the cake looks like it was made by Frankenstein.

Ugh, Scenarios? That's Not Very Innovative...

Previously we have challenged what is truly innovative (depending on how you parse the definition, maybe nothing!), and the challenges of systems wide innovation. We can now introduce 4 possible scenarios (among many, many others) to begin to conceptualize what the future of innovation looks like:

Baseline. The baseline scenario has organizations, governments, and economies continuing to muddle through. Some continue to sub optimize and exist, others innovate to various degrees, others are shape shifters, able to leap from one new industry to another, evolving as they go along. Over time, we become more fluent in the efficiency and quality of innovation activities, using such measurements as research quotients (RQ), developed by Anne Marie Knott, that measure innovation inputs and outputs to gauge success. Innovation as disruption is still seen as the gold standard, though large, mature firms still struggle with whether to embrace or suppress these disruptions. Innovation is still largely situated.

Systems-Bound Mutual Self-Interest: A greater understanding of systems, and systems literacy, coupled with virtual and software based platforms and physical innovative cross-disciplinary spaces point to less sub optimization and unproductive situated innovation. Instead, organizations will bond together in mutual self-interest (perhaps making some a bit uneasy as self-organization looks a lot like vertical integration and monopolization). Definitions of competition and anti-trust will be rewritten and new measurements of social good will come to eclipse GDP as the primary measurement of innovation and economic health.

Double-Down on Sub-Optimization and Quick Profit. The insatiable thirst for quarterly profits points to a future of sub optimization that shows no signs of disappearing. In an effort to stimulate the real economy, governments implement varying policies of charging demurrage on the financial market, charging fees or taxing capital that isn't being used in "productive" ways. This will increase available capital for reinvestment. However, instead of increasing innovation and productivity, it could simply "feed the beast" of sub optimization. Especially when coupled with the relentless focus on quarterly returns, on "maximizing value". In a world where capital must be reinvested in the firm, the resultant behavior could involve a great deal of tire spinning, or more precisely, short-term cycles of excessive value extraction meant to replicate share buy-back schemes and large dividend payouts. This, coupled with rapid rise and fall "fad" industries, make for rapid boom-bust cycles globally. Think of it as shifting the burden on overdrive.

The Rapid S-Curve Economy. Organizations become increasingly amorphous, shape shifters that are constantly seeking out new emergent industries, colonizing them rapidly, then moving on once the industry matures. And the maturity of the industries is also rapid. Organizations become almost nomadic. With either large or scarce reserves of capital for innovation and expansion, organizations move to rapidly create and capitalize on opportunities; one or two players prove successful and monopolize the space; the rest move on to find greener pastures.

What to do? The answer may be in the form of government policy. Governments are still the primary investor in risky innovative endeavours. When will investment programs and structures be put in place to invest in systems wide innovation? Even if it is still sub optimized within the nation-state?

Perhaps this is all just an elaborate way of saying that innovation is messy, often fails, and even when successful we can't be sure of what positive and negative externalities it will cause. Ultimately, sub optimization is inherently a product of innovation. By correcting one problem we create others. Not all problems are created equal, of course, and we would prefer to have certain problems over others – for example, all the side-effects associated with medications we choose are an unfortunate but necessary trade off. We are both selfish in the sense that we view progress from our own situated perspective, and we are utilitarian in the sense that we generally hope that any negative outcomes of innovation will be less than the derived benefit.

We are left with a future where the nature and impact, not to mention the consistency and payback, of innovation, creating results by doing new things, is unclear. Will we move towards increased sub optimization or will we create and adopt the social technologies we need to generate deep structural results?

Transitioning to a New Form of Innovation

For those frustrated with the traditional tools and challenges of transformational innovation in a complex world, focus has turned to systems innovation. But does systems innovation address the underlying problem of sub optimization? Using the oft-quoted Einstein, "No problem can be solved from the same level of consciousness that created it."

What lies beneath our systems? Causal Layer Analysis, or CLA, provides some insight. For those unfamiliar with this concept, a brief example of the futures technique. At the top is what is known as the Litany. Imagine a headline in the newspaper: "Lawmakers Punished at the Ballot Box for Proposing Tax Increases". In essence, tax increases are almost never popular despite some fairly substantial benefits. Litany is the noise at the top.

Below Litany is the Pattern level, in which we see tax trends (typically, decreases, especially in the corporate world). Beneath the Pattern level is the System/Structural level, in which political parties, nominations, lobbying groups, political donations, tax laws, etc., exist that shape the patterns of decreasing taxation. We would typically stop here in the more "woke" realms of innovation, system innovation. But in the CLA model, there are 2 more layers.

Underneath our tax systems, we have Worldviews. For our example, we will adopt a Modernist worldview: "Work hard and your life will get better". And, underpinning all of this is the Myth or Organizing Metaphor. In this case, let us go with the American Dream: "Anyone can succeed."

So, to play this all back: The organizing metaphor of the American Dream manifests in the modernist worldview of hard work and progress, which crystalizes into the political and financial systems, which create patterns of ever decreasing taxes (because we work hard for our money and if you have no money you must be lazy), which flare up into an event where a small group of pitiful politicians actually tries to do something about it.

How do we overcome sub optimization at the systems level? Narrative Innovation. By digging to the deepest layers of our collective existence. Not in the way that narrative innovation has perhaps been used before; using stories to generate new innovation. But rather the inverse: innovating the stories. Our underlying archetypal stories need to change in order to create true "systems wide" innovation.

This change is not merely a reworking of plot points, but a re-conception of the structure of our archetypal narratives. The French philosopher Deleuze asserts that we have moved from a moral existence to an aesthetic one. Within this move, there are Five Dualities, one of which is the move from Idea to Image. Much has been written about "images of the future", and, perhaps, before we had images of the future we had ideas of the future. But as Fred Polak noted more than 50 years ago, our images are in decline. While we have focused some energy on regenerating our images to guide us towards a new future, perhaps it is too late? Perhaps images are no longer the vehicles, the beacons of our future? Perhaps we have moved into a new form of existence? From moral to aesthetic to something else altogether. And our underlying organizing metaphors must also evolve, must also be innovated. From ideas of the future to images of the future to (you fill in the blank).

The Make Believe Economy: The Performative Nature of Scarcity

Jean-Paul Sartre wrote "The essence of reality is scarcity. There isn't enough love in the world, enough food, enough justice, enough time in life. To gain any sense of satisfaction in our life we must go in to heady conflict with the forces of scarcity."

We have explored the future of the real economy from a number of perspectives. We now turn to a key ingredient of the real economy, probably the most fundamental tenant of modern economics: scarcity. Or, put another way, supply and demand. Seen through this lens supply and demand can be reconfigured as the tension between the real and the unreal. Supply can be real or unreal. Ditto for demand. In the absence of perfect information, we are left with an elaborate economic performance.

Performance studies, an interdisciplinary discipline that uses the frame of performance to view the world, classifies the blurring of the real and unreal, between reality and performance, as "Make believe". Put another way, we create belief through performance. One example is the ways in which we "perform" stereotypical roles of ourselves. We come to embody ways of being that aren't really our true selves, but a blending of who we really are with the make believe societal perceptions of who we ought to be.

In the post-scarcity world, forecasted sometime in the next 50 years, competitive advantage becomes a "make believe" process by which conventional rules of scarcity can still be applied. Where a "post-scarcity" economy would appear to be a desired future goal there is nothing to suggest that our penchant for performances of scarcity won't simply prompt us to create ever evolving and elaborate domains of scarcity. As self-replication becomes ubiquitous, human desires could turn to that which defies self-replication. We want what everyone else has until we've got it – then we want something else. Where the bulk of business activities today focus on overcoming some form or another of scarcity (not enough cheap labour, not enough materials, etc.) in the future, there could be a far more concerted effort to stimulate scarcity. Scarcity = real, and real = profit. Simply being "real" will have its own market cache. In a post-scarcity economy, the performance of scarcity will become the de facto marketing campaign for any business.

Evidence of this shift is already well underway. Witness the plethora of food movements, most of which fit broadly under the category of "real food". Organic, local, Non-GMO. In short, food that is typically scarcer and therefore more "real" than other, abundant foods.

There is a danger that the ongoing performance of scarcity beguiles us into seeing scarce goods as better than non-scarce goods. Our culture of consumption and rituals to colonize and monetize show few signs of faltering. If we want to move beyond the real economy, beyond scarcity, the technology we focus on will only get us halfway to our goal. Unfortunately, we still have to change our habits, how we act, and move into a new form of capitalist culture. It will still be an elaborate performance of make believe, but at least it will be sustainable and equitable.

The World is turning into a Pumpkin Patch

To the best of my recollection, when I was young my family only went to the pumpkin patch once. Every year we would beg to go. Every year my father would say "no" and explain to us the minute difference between the cost of a store bought pumpkin, and the cost of going to the pumpkin patch. Plus, transportation costs. Compound interest and so forth… Of course, he preferred a third option: no pumpkin at all.

But what, exactly, is the allure of a pumpkin patch? It's usually raining, cold. Certainly, from an economic perspective, grabbing one at the grocery store is cheaper, more efficient, probably better for the environment. In "Emotionally Durable Design", Jonathan Chapman turns to social psychologist Erich Fromm, invoking the consumption relationship between incorporation and possession in ritual acts of cannibalism. To consume another human being, or animal, is to acquire their strength or courage, or whatever power they possess that is deemed accessible to acquisition.

This insight points to the evolution of an ongoing trend: A psychological and consumer shift away from "having" into "being", one in which we focus our economic energies on immersing ourselves in the experience, a cannibalistic form of possession.

"Authentic experiences" are a case in point. These experiences at their most pure are serendipitous, original, unmediated, and have a profound, lasting impact on individuals. Here, perhaps, is a clue as to the future of the real economy: where ecological and cultural resources are extracted experientially versus a coordinated process meant to maximize efficiency.

Think of the global economy shifting to an unwieldy version of what we might call "The Pumpkin Patch Scenario", the expansion of unmediated, or low-mediated, cultural exploitation. Foraging would be an example of this; much like those who set out "off the beaten path" to find spaces uncolonized by tourism. The "being" of the experience supersedes the "having" of the object. The economic transaction is dependent upon the experience of the pumpkin patch and not on the pumpkin itself.

Why might this shift be happening? Perhaps because of the over-commercialization and manipulation of emotion, the synthetic and scripted quality of our products and experiences. As design increasingly mediates our experiences we must wander further afield to escape into the unrefined. All of this will have dire consequences on the climate, as our consumption patterns become more emergent and esoteric.

While this turn from "having" to "being" is well underway, whether it manifests in a virtual "being" or a "real" being is yet to be determined. The most likely scenario is a mixing of the two, in which we chose to have a virtual and physical presence. An exaggerated version of today. One in which the more deeply we immerse ourselves in the synthetic, the more invasively we mine the authentic when we come up for air.

But a more radical shift could be under way. One in which citizens choose to primarily inhabit either the synthetic or the authentic. In the future, our economy could be divided along wholly new lines: instead of developed and developing economies, we could have those who inhabit the virtual economy, those who inhabit the physical economy, and those who cross between. What would an economy look like where consumers are located by their chosen, or imposed, economically situated "being-ness", versus traditional socio-economic boundaries?

Fake It Till You Make It

Previously we have explored various ways in which the real economy may or may not be real in the future, utilizing the concept of hyperstition, the combination of "hyper" and "superstition", which refers to the process of ideas becoming reality in our culture. More specifically, how new realities manifest in the economy.

While perhaps the academic study of hyperstition and its effects and influence on late-capitalism is relatively new, the conceptual underpinnings are not. One of the most well-known lines in the Bible is "And the word became flesh and dwelt among us" (English Standard for those wondering). In our current age, the capacity for words to dwell among us, in the various forms of social media in general, twitter in particular, and our latent inventiveness in turning ideas into reality, has led to a powerful and reinforcing loop between the word and flesh.

The myriad ways in which this has influenced our economic systems have been explored, though far from exhaustively. We've looked at the nefarious means by which late-capitalism will continue to mine the nooks and crannies of everyday life for growth opportunities, including trauma-related world building in the form of imaginary paracosm economies, and the incredible ecological strain of consumers shifting from "having" to "being" consumption patterns. In the virtual realm we've considered whether AI entrepreneurs pumping out transient products and services will cause our much admired entrepreneur to become extinct along with those who face the future challenges of virtual foraging. Finally, we've delved into the implications of the grand performance of scarcity in a post-scarcity world, the hamster-wheel of sub optimization brought on by situated innovation and, of course, back to where we started our journey with pigeon Ponzi schemes going up in smoke.

Of course, our fiction to reality process is far from linear. And it is far from monolithic. With the most recent rise of nationalism, with left and right in a constant oppositional state of becoming far-left and far-right, we've also seen the proliferation of folk economics. This rejection of globalism for localism, whether practical or not, has likewise bred a plethora of local, culturally and economically ingrained hyperstitional realities. Reality and economics is now situational. The economy is both great and terrible.

We have been referred to grandly as "The Weather Makers". Perhaps of greater concern is our inconsistent ability to be "The Reality Makers". Still far from clear is how this will manifest in the future, where reality is customizable and up for debate.

As for the Pigeon King story I began with, I recently attended a play in rural Ontario, a matinee production, called "The Pigeon King", based on the true story in which a man built a Ponzi scheme empire selling pigeons. Or, perhaps, he was just a bad businessman. Regardless, economic abstractions had given way to tangible pigeons, which had now given way to a theatrical performance. Fact had come full circle back to fiction. After the play finished, the performers took their bow. But we weren't done yet. The performers encouraged us to open our programs. In the program was a folded paper pigeon. They told us to pull out the pigeons and then, on the count of three, we launched our pigeons into the rafters of the theatre. A theatre full of old people, laughing, suddenly children again. A sad flock of paper pigeons trying to take flight, sputtering out, before being snatched back up and tossed a few feet further. Up on stage the actors and the musicians watched. The audience and performers had switched roles. I noticed the fiddler. He didn't play now. Just watches us. Content.

Adam Cowart

Is Another Great Power War Inevitable?

1. Is Another Great-Power War Inevitable?

2. What's So Great About the Great Powers?

3. War: What Is It Good For?

4. With Competition Like This, Who Needs Conflict?

5. Should we learn to stop worrying and love the bomb?

6. Why aren't nukes ever enough?

7. What sparks could ignite the next great-power conflagration?

8. What profit is there in great-power war?

9. Can international institutions constrain great-power conflict?

10. Can the world be made safe through democracy?

11. What if anarchy is merely what we make of it?

12. Is the United States still indispensable?

Is Another Great-Power War Inevitable?

"Anarchy places a premium on foresight." – Kenneth Waltz

A century ago, with the world embroiled in what was then naively dubbed the "war to end all wars," few people imagined a second global conflagration igniting just a generation later. Since the end of World War II, however, humanity has experienced over seven decades of relative peace, with the frequency of war deaths trending sharply downward throughout this period. This is largely attributable to the Cold War between the United States and Soviet Union, a standoff that spawned numerous proxy conflicts but never turned truly hot. It remains to be seen whether the ongoing re-emergence of a multipolar world, with potentially several states capable of exerting influence on a global scale, will lead to yet more wars among these so-called great powers.

There are good reasons to fear a return to great-power conflict. Warfare has been endemic to the human condition since the dawn of civilization, and remains the ultimate way of resolving conflicts among states even in the modern era. World affairs are inherently anarchic, with states pursuing their own advantages in a Hobbesian struggle of each against all. While the weak may occasionally band together to balance would-be hegemons, the prevailing self-help system of international relations features no permanent friends or enemies, just interests. "Countries have always competed for wealth and security, and the competition has often led to conflict," the late neo-realist scholar Kenneth Waltz noted. "Why should the future be different from the past?"

Indeed, war has accompanied the rise and fall of great powers throughout recorded history. In his classic account of the Peloponnesian War, Greek historian Thucydides concluded that the growth of Athenian power and the fear this inspired in then-dominant Sparta made war between these city-states inevitable. This dynamic, which political scientist Graham Allison calls the "Thucydides Trap," has ensnared rising and established powers in more than a dozen wars over the last 500 years—and it threatens to do so again as other states challenge the United States for global influence.

Such systemic, structural factors are not the only aspects of international relations that can drive states towards armed conflict. Marxists argue that capitalism compels the core, industrialized powers to compete for dominance as they exploit peripheral countries for labor and raw materials. Political scientist Samuel Huntington suggested it is culture—rather than ideology, politics, or economics—that is shaping patterns of conflict, with the Western belief in the universality of its values leading to clashes with rival civilizations. Constructivists similarly believe ideas shape international relations, as each state perceives world events in its own peculiar way.

So why should the future be different from the past? With nearly 200 sovereign states around the globe, it seems inevitable that at least some of them will come into conflict in the coming decades—and great powers will occasionally intervene, if only to enforce international law or for some other ostensibly noble purpose. Yet it is far from certain that these great powers will again come to blows with each other, for several reasons. While anarchy will continue to characterize international relations for the foreseeable future, a number of developments—including nuclear deterrence, globalization of trade and investment, relevant international institutions, shifting social norms, and widespread competition below the threshold of war—are incrementally reducing the likelihood of another great-power conflict. Will these trends be enough to prevent the eventual outbreak of World War III?

What's So Great About the Great Powers?

Before we can answer the question of whether another great-power war is inevitable, we should first clarify what constitutes greatness in the context of international relations. Scholars have debated this issue over the years, focusing primarily on military strength underpinned by economic vitality—which in turn are functions of population, resource endowment, and territorial expanse. A state's political system can also contribute to its great-power rank, especially when it mobilizes its potential in pursuit of global interests. And of course, a state's ability to shape the preferences of others through diplomacy, culture, and values—its soft power—augments its military and economic instruments of national power.

Given all that, the number of prospective great powers will remain quite small through the middle of the 21st century—with the world's sole remaining superpower continuing to top the list. Although China and India will likely overtake the United States as the world's largest economies by 2050, America's steadily growing population should compensate for lacklustre growth. Washington shows no sign of retreating into isolationism as it did after the First World War, and it will almost certainly continue investing in formidable military forces to defend its expansive interests around the globe, as well as exercising a significant—if increasingly contested—role in institutions ranging from the United Nations and North Atlantic Treaty Organization to the World Bank and International Monetary Fund.

By mid-century, however, America will no longer be the world's unrivalled hegemon. The People's Republic of China has already surpassed the United States in gross domestic product at purchasing power parity, and this lead will only widen in the coming decades regardless of the Middle Kingdom's impending demographic decline. The People's Liberation Army is emerging as a near-peer competitor to the U.S. military, bolstering China's increasingly assertive foreign policy ambitions in Asia and around the world. Frustrated by U.S.-dominated international institutions, China is developing a rival framework to advance its foreign-policy ambitions.

If China is slowly re-emerging as a great power after a century and a half of foreign domination, the Russian Federation clings to delusions of Soviet grandeur despite the collapse of its empire, economy, and political system within the past three decades. Russia retains an enormous landmass and a wealth of natural resources, but it has less than half the population of the USSR—and it is expected to shrink further in the coming decades. Nevertheless, Russia is projected to remain the world's sixth largest economy through mid-century—its overreliance on oil and gas exploitation notwithstanding—and Moscow will remain capable of fielding ever-more sophisticated military forces and projecting power across much of the globe. Moreover, unlike the Chinese, Russians can recall what it was like to be a superpower within living memory, and their leaders are determined to restore the Eurasian bear to (what they believe is) its rightful place in the international community.

While China and Russia are revisionist states challenging the U.S.-dominated international order, several other former great powers are less likely to disturb the status quo. Japan's demographic decline and meagre economic growth do not bode well for its future influence in a region increasingly dominated by its arch-rival, China. While Germany's trajectory is similar to Japan, its influence is amplified by its membership in the European Union, whose combined population and economic output will continue to surpass America's even after Britain exits the bloc. If Germany, France, and other EU member states were to renew their quest for an ever closer union by further pooling sovereignty in the foreign and security policy domains, it is not farfetched to imagine a European super-state could one day emerge as a great power alongside the United States—or even its rival, should America's NATO commitments waver.

Of the remaining states whose economic and demographic growth ought to inspire great power aspirations, none are likely to overcome their internal weaknesses or emerge from the shadow of powerful neighbours anytime soon. India, for example, will boast the world's largest population and second-largest economy by mid-century, but its unwieldy political system and China's regional dominance will limit its great-power prospects.

Ultimately, what makes great powers great depends not only on what they bring to the table, but also on which other states have already claimed a seat. The United States, China, Russia, and (perhaps) the EU will continue to crowd out most regional rivals through a combination of economic strength, military prowess, and soft-power appeal, while leveraging their privileged positions in international institutions like the UN Security Council to advance their interests. Rogue regimes, terrorist and criminal networks, and transnational corporations and other nongovernmental organizations will undoubtedly nudge international relations this way or that, but it is the great powers who will continue writing the rules of the game.

War: What Is It Good For?

Anarchy is a feature of our international system. Not a bug. With no supranational authority capable of policing relations between sovereign states, competition for resources and influence can naturally lead to conflict. Great powers will sometimes resort to war—despite the risk and expense this entails—when their other, non-military instruments of national power come up short. As Carl von Clausewitz famously observed nearly two centuries ago, war is simply a continuation of politics by other means—namely, acts of violence to compel opponents to fulfil one's will. The nature of war hasn't changed much in the intervening years; even as armed conflict has become less endemic in world affairs.

If we were to construct a taxonomy of reasons great powers wage war, it might closely resemble Maslow's hierarchy of needs. Regime survival in the face of an existential threat is the most fundamental excuse for conflict, followed closely by the protection of national sovereignty or territorial integrity. Great powers may also go to war to preserve or expand their spheres of influence over less-powerful neighbours, while the defence of allies against a mutual adversary lies higher up the proverbial pyramid. At the top of the hierarchy we would find enforcement of international law and humanitarian intervention, arguably the most enlightened—or rather, least indefensible—pretexts for war.

Whatever its causes, however, war is always an ugly business, and great powers have long sought to constrain its excesses by codifying laws governing armed conflict. In the aftermath of World War II, the victorious Allied Powers even resolved "to save succeeding generations from the scourge of war" once and for all by establishing the United Nations, whose charter provided mechanisms for the pacific settlement of disputes and maintenance of international peace and security. Yet the UN Charter also enshrined the inherent right of states to defend themselves from armed attack, and granted the great powers of the day—in their roles as permanent members of the UN Security Council—sweeping authority to determine when a state of war exists; intervene militarily to restore the peace; and prevent the UN from acting against their interests. Such concessions were necessary to gain buy-in for the UN project, but this design flaw has guaranteed that future generations would continue to experience the scourge of war.

The question of what, exactly, constitutes war has taken on increased urgency in recent decades, as combatants have found ever more innovative ways to wreak havoc. Article 5 of the North Atlantic Treaty, for example, commits NATO members to consider an armed attack against any one of them as an attack on them all. Yet the only time in its history the Alliance has invoked this provision was not in response to a conventional military assault, but rather after the 9/11 terrorist attacks. In 2014, the Alliance further warned that cyberattacks could also trigger Article 5 if they reached a threshold that threatened NATO's prosperity, security, or stability. Meanwhile, NATO has quietly dropped the qualifier "armed" when describing its Article 5 obligations in most of its communiqués—a tacit admission, perhaps, that war can come in all shapes and sizes.

Indeed, while all the great powers maintain formidable forces capable of conducting offensive military operations, they are also fielding new tools and techniques to compel opponents to fulfil their will short of armed conflict—that is, without egregiously violating international law or crossing a collective-defence threshold. Consequently, future wars may not reflect the thinking of Clausewitz so much as the ancient Chinese strategist Sun Tzu, who wrote: "The supreme art of war is to subdue the enemy without fighting."

With Competition Like This, Who Needs Conflict?

"If you call what's going on now a hybrid war, let it be hybrid war. It doesn't matter: It's war." – Dmitry Peskov, Kremlin spokesperson

What if the great powers really could subdue their enemies without fighting, as Sun Tzu suggested? This appears to be what Russian agents were up to in 2016 when they allegedly meddled in America's presidential elections. According to the U.S. intelligence community and federal prosecutors, Moscow's goals were to undermine public faith in democracy and influence the selection of the next U.S. commander-in-chief, presumably with the aim of weakening a superpower rival—or better yet, installing a favoured candidate in the White House. Russians apparently were up to similar tricks in the latest French, German, and Montenegrin elections as well.

Then again, the United States and its allies are hardly innocent when it comes to interfering in other countries' affairs—so it should come as no surprise that Moscow blames the West for much of the world's instability, from Arab Spring uprisings to "colour revolutions" across the former Soviet Union. In 2013, Gen. Valeriy Gerasimov, chief of the Russian general staff, framed these turbulent events as a new form of warfare, where political, economic, informational, humanitarian, and other non-military measures are often more effective than traditional weapons. The very rules of war have changed, he concluded, and Russia's military must adapt accordingly.

The Kremlin has clearly embraced these modern rules of war in recent years, pursuing an aggressive, whole-of-government approach to achieving its foreign policy goals while avoiding escalation into full-blown state-on-state conflicts. This strategy of indirect action typically begins with so-called "information confrontation," a combination of old-fashioned propaganda and modern cyber operations to shape perceptions and manipulate the behaviour of target audiences. Russia's intelligence services might then mix it up with subversive "active measures," while the military and its proxies—ethnic compatriots, private military contractors, or even "little green men"—stand ready to up the ante while obscuring Moscow's involvement.

Not to be outdone, China also updated its military doctrine to incorporate non-military means of influence in 2003. The People's Liberation Army's "three warfares" strategy—encompassing public opinion, psychological, and legal warfare—is intended to control public narratives and influence perceptions to advance China's interests while compromising the ability of opponents to respond. This approach offers China a new form of "non-kinetic" weaponry that can be combined in highly synergistic ways. For example, to advance its territorial claims in the East and South China Seas, Beijing is advancing spurious legal arguments, deploying civilian flotillas, and broadcasting propaganda portraying itself as a victim of foreign powers. Sun Tzu would be proud.

There is debate in national security circles over what to call these new forms of warfare—and whether they are really all that new. Pundits have coined terms such as "grey zone conflicts" and "hybrid warfare" to describe what others chalk up to time-honoured doctrinal concepts like information operations and irregular warfare. The 2018 U.S. National Defence Strategy offered yet another buzz phrase for this phenomenon: "competition short of armed conflict."

Whatever we call it, there is no doubt that non-military methods of warfare are becoming more commonplace, for a variety of reasons. Compared to traditional combat operations, they are relatively inexpensive, deceptively innocuous, and difficult to attribute, particularly in the cyber domain. They also carry limited risk of escalation, as even the most audacious provocations seldom trigger an armed response—especially against a nuclear power. Perhaps most importantly, these subtle, indirect approaches can sometimes affect strategic centres of gravity—such as government decision-making and political legitimacy—that are difficult to target directly with military force. Future advances in communications technology, big-data analytics, and artificial intelligence will only further enable such competition below the threshold of conflict.

This is certainly a worrying trend, as these tactics have the potential to exacerbate social divisions, undermine confidence in democratic governance, and blur distinctions between civilian and military combatants and targets. On the other hand, the more confident great powers are in their ability to secure national interests through non-military means, the more likely they are to pursue less violent and risky courses of action. In other words, competition short of conflict could very well reduce the risk of future great-power wars.

Should we learn to stop worrying and love the bomb?

"There's no such thing as a winnable war, it's a lie we don't believe anymore." – Sting, "Russians"

The Cold War was a scary time for citizens on both sides of the Iron Curtain. The United States and the Soviet Union each wielded massive nuclear arsenals with the capacity to destroy the world many times over—and they came perilously close to unleashing these awful weapons on more than one occasion. Yet for all the anxiety this decades-long standoff entailed, it fostered an uneasy peace between the superpowers.

Once the United States demonstrated the terrible potential of the atom bomb at the end of World War II, it was only a matter of time before the Soviet Union and other would-be great powers sought to acquire their own nukes. By the 1960s, the two superpowers had so many warheads—deliverable by a triad of airborne, land-based, and submarine platforms managed by robust command-and-control systems—that neither side could launch first without precipitating a devastating counterattack. The era of mutually assured destruction had begun.

While such strategic deterrence has produced a degree of stability in international affairs, it also creates perverse disincentives for arms control. Any developments that might undermine this suicide pact—for example, by defeating incoming weapons (anti-ballistic missile systems), overwhelming missile defences (multiple independently targetable re-entry vehicles), or making limited regional nuclear exchanges more plausible (intermediate-range nuclear forces)—are seen by the other side as dangerously provocative. Even the dramatic cutbacks of the Strategic Arms Reduction Treaty and follow-on New START left Moscow and Washington with more than enough firepower to obliterate each other. In the nuclear arms race, at least, Russia remains every bit as powerful as its American rival.

Yet while mutually assured destruction makes large-scale wars between nuclear powers less likely, it paradoxically permits them to engage in smaller conflicts without fear of escalation. During the Cold War, U.S. nuclear strategy quickly evolved to deemphasize massive retaliation in favour of more flexible responses as the superpowers found themselves embroiled in numerous proxy conflicts. This stability-instability paradox also encourages nuclear proliferation among lesser powers seeking to guarantee their own regime survival. Although small nuclear stockpiles with limited delivery means may deter regional rivals (e.g. India/Pakistan), they offer no guarantee against a determined great power—and a rogue regime's pursuit of the bomb can just as easily provoke crippling sanctions and pre-emptive war.

While the end of the Cold War reduced the risk of global thermonuclear war, it hasn't done much to curb the enthusiasm of great powers to maintain and enhance their strategic forces. Shortly after the Pentagon released its 2018 nuclear posture review calling for new low-yield warheads and sea-launched cruise missiles, the Russian president publicly revealed several other weapons under development. Meanwhile, China continues to modernize its much smaller but quite capable triad as a hedge against first-use by its great-power rivals—and has likely reconsidered its previous, destabilizing support for Pakistani and North Korean nuclear ambitions.

Not surprisingly, efforts to ban the bomb—including the 2017 UN Treaty on the Prohibition of Nuclear Weapons—enjoy almost no support among nuclear powers and America's NATO allies. Still, with the majority of the world's states, the ocean floor, and even outer space now legally designated nuclear-weapons-free zones, there is a growing international consensus that nuclear warfare is beyond the pale. Despite some backsliding in recent years, the great powers are generally committed to arms control and non-proliferation as a means of preserving strategic stability—and even junior members of the nuclear club have existential incentives to behave responsibly. But whether or not you love the bomb, there's not much point worrying about what's become a necessary evil in our anarchic international system, which will continue deterring great-power conflict for the foreseeable future.

Why aren't nukes ever enough?

For all their destructive potential, nuclear weapons ushered in an unprecedented era of global stability after 1945, deterring the great powers from the kinds of internecine conflicts that risk their mutual destruction. But this period hasn't been entirely peaceful, either, as states and non-state actors have sporadically waged more limited wars the old-fashioned way—that is, utilizing "conventional" weapons—whenever they calculate the odds of nuclear escalation are low. Consequently, powers great and small have continued to arm themselves with military capabilities of ever-increasing speed and lethality, determined to gain a decisive advantage on some future battlefield—an unfortunate function of survival in our anarchic international system.

For much of the Cold War, the United States made little effort to match the Soviet Union's massive conventional-warfare superiority in Europe, calculating that its nuclear arsenal would be enough to offset any Soviet military advantage. Beginning in the late 1970s, however, the Pentagon embarked on a new offset strategy incorporating technological breakthroughs in precision-guided munitions, radar-evading stealth technology aircraft, and space-based communications and navigation. Rather than rely on the traditional American way of war—attrition and annihilation—this revolution in military affairs allowed relatively small numbers of highly nimble American and allied forces to defeat numerically superior adversaries, as dramatically demonstrated during such operations as Desert Storm (1991) and Iraqi Freedom (2003), while sharply reducing civilian casualties and collateral damage.

Some scholars attribute the collapse of the Soviet Union in part to its failed efforts to keep up with the West in this expensive, high-tech arms race—and for decades afterward the United States had no peers in terms of conventional military capabilities. But a funny thing happened on the way to American global hegemony: while Washington diverted resources away from cutting-edge investments after 9/11, Moscow and Beijing slowly but surely began closing the capability gap through a combination of indigenous know-how, industrial espionage, and lessons learned from U.S. military operations. In recent years, Russia and China have developed increasingly effective air defence systems to blunt America's signature warfighting advantage, and deployed sophisticated missile systems on a variety of platforms to complicate U.S. ground and maritime operations near their territory. Such anti-access, area-denial measures complement their markedly improved power-projection capabilities now on display in Syria and the South China Sea, respectively.

Not to be outdone, the U.S. Department of Defence recently embarked on a third offset strategy to harness innovations in artificial intelligence, automation, additive manufacturing, and other fields. While traditional weapons acquisition processes have become increasingly unaffordable—with more and more money spent procuring fewer and fewer high-end aircraft, ships, and armoured vehicles—this latest approach hopes to reduce costs by disaggregating marquee platforms into more specialized networked systems leveraging off-the-shelf commercial technology. Of course, this same technology is accessible to America's rivals as well, suggesting U.S. forces will soon need to develop new defences against the very drone swarms and other "futuristic" weaponry they are currently developing, in a seemingly never-ending cycle.

Unfortunately, such military modernization has the potential to make great-power conflict more likely, their credible nuclear deterrents notwithstanding. Both Russia and China perceive America's superior conventional capabilities—coupled with its expanding anti-ballistic missile networks in Europe and Asia—as destabilizing, since they could facilitate pre-emptive U.S. attacks targeting their nuclear arsenals. Meanwhile, each country is developing its own expeditionary forces capable of quickly seizing nearby territory, then (theoretically) holding out against an anticipated U.S.-led conventional counterattack—which may embolden them to resolve a greater variety of regional disputes militarily, especially where they judge the United States unwilling to intervene at the risk of nuclear war.

This combination of mutual distrust and localized military parity is increasing the likelihood of strategic miscalculation, and undermining the logic of nuclear deterrence that has constrained great-power competition for nearly three-quarters of a century. While it remains unlikely that the United States, Russia, or China will launch large-scale attacks on each other in the coming decades, they could very well become embroiled in regional conflicts that devolve into direct military confrontation among the great powers—conflicts with the potential for a much wider global conflagration.

What sparks could ignite the next great-power conflagration?

America's great-power rivals are increasingly pursuing strategic ends through non-military means, betting that competition short of conflict will advance their interests without risking nuclear annihilation. Yet they are also gearing up to project military force abroad, and defend themselves should the United States intervene to defend its interests and allies. This raises the very real possibility that Russian or Chinese adventurism—and miscalculations over American willingness or ability to respond militarily—could inadvertently trigger the next great-power war. Unfortunately, growing doubts about longstanding U.S. commitments to its allies and international norms are making this tragic outcome far more likely.

Russia has re-emerged in the past decade as a formidable military power, capable of defeating neighbouring states such as Georgia and Ukraine while seizing the initiative farther afield in Syria. Its theatre ballistic missiles and sophisticated air and coastal defence systems dominate the Black Sea and Baltic regions, posing a worrying threat to America's NATO allies. Similarly, the People's Republic of China has vastly improved its offensive capabilities in recent years, projecting naval power far beyond its littoral areas while holding its renegade offshore province, Taiwan, at ever-greater risk.

These developments have substantially increased the likelihood of American forces coming into conflict with their great-power counterparts. For example, not long after Russian mercenaries launched an ill-fated attack on a U.S. outpost in Syria, the United States and Russia nearly come to blows over the Syrian regime's use of chemical weapons. Just a month later, China deployed a nuclear-capable bomber to the disputed Paracel Islands, then dispatched warships to challenge the U.S. Navy's freedom of navigation in the region. As such brinkmanship becomes more common, the likelihood of a serious—and potentially escalatory—military confrontation will only grow.

This problem is particularly acute wherever the United States maintains alliances within its rivals' historical spheres of influence. In Europe, Moscow could quickly defeat the meagre NATO forces forward-deployed to the Baltic States—former Soviet republics sandwiched between mainland Russia and its Kaliningrad exclave—while making it exceedingly difficult for the United States and its allies to retake this territory without triggering nuclear war. Meanwhile in Asia, Beijing has set a mid-century deadline for national reunification, with the People's Liberation Army reportedly planning to accomplish this goal as early as 2020. The PLA is already poised to overwhelm

Taiwanese defences with little warning, and disrupt U.S. carrier and airbase operations as far away as Okinawa and Guam through a combination of kinetic, cyber, and electronic warfare. In both cases, America's near-peer adversaries are positioned to seize the initiative in their own backyards while severely complicating Washington's ability to come to the aid of its allies.

All of this presupposes, of course, that the United States remains fully committed to its far-flung network of alliances, which have been a cornerstone of its foreign policy success since World War II. The 2016 election of a U.S. commander-in-chief who repeatedly questions the value of NATO and other foreign entanglements, however, has fundamentally challenged assumptions of American resolve. President Trump's pronouncements naturally undermine confidence in U.S. security guarantees, and this growing uncertainty may eventually embolden Russia or China to call America's bluff. The ramifications of such a gamble would be catastrophic: if the U.S. military responds as promised, it would plunge the world into the next great-power war; if it does not, the international system that has underpinned global peace and prosperity for the better part of a century would come to an ignominious end. Either way, the future is shaping up to be a much different place than the "Pax Americana" of yesteryear.

What profit is there in great-power war?

In 1999, American journalist Thomas Friedman penned his notorious "Golden Arches Theory of Conflict Prevention," positing that no countries with McDonald's restaurants had ever fought a war against each other. Critics quickly noted that the presence of this ubiquitous American fast-food chain hadn't stopped the U.S. invasion of Panama a decade earlier, nor would it preclude NATO from bombing Serbia (1999), the Kargil War between India and Pakistan (1999), Israel's second Lebanon war (2006), or Russian incursions into Georgia (2008) and Ukraine (2014-present). But even if Friedman's pop theory is bunk, it echoes an established maxim of international relations: globalization makes countries so economically interdependent, they can't afford to wage war very intensely for very long.

English journalist Norman Angell popularized this argument nearly a century earlier, dismissing the supposed economic benefits of war as "the great illusion." The commercial systems of Europe and America had become so complicated, Angell wrote in 1909, that it is impossible for one nation "to enrich itself by subjugating, or imposing its will by force on another." The world was then experiencing a remarkable era of globalization, with freely flowing capital and labour producing unprecedented prosperity, and the European powers had few incentives to risk this arrangement through war.

Nevertheless, the continent soon plunged headlong into conflict—followed by an even more cataclysmic sequel a generation later—and it would be several more decades before international trade and finance fully returned to pre-World War I levels. Although Angell went on to win the Nobel Peace Prize for his idealistic views, it wasn't until 1950 that Robert Schuman, the French foreign minister who championed the European Coal and Steel Community, offered a practical vision to "make war not only unthinkable but materially impossible." The free movement of goods, services, capital, and people within what is now known as the European Union has indeed facilitated peace among its members ever since.

Of course, neither the EU nor its constituent states are counted among the world's great powers nowadays, while those that are—the United States, China, and Russia—haven't achieved anything close to this level of economic interdependence. Although the sheer volume of Chinese wealth invested in the U.S. economy, which is itself highly vulnerable to disruption by Beijing, ought to be sufficient to deter military conflict, there are worrying signs that this mutually profitable arrangement is breaking down. Washington has recently abandoned its longstanding support for globalization in favor of trade wars with its closest allies and fiercest competitors, while the Middle Kingdom's commitment to build a world-class military by 2050 suggests its foreign policy ambitions will soon catch up with its global economic dominance. Russia, for its part, is far less integrated into the world economy, while its oil and gas customers can't easily switch to other suppliers in the event of conflict, reducing Moscow's incentives to curb its aggressive behaviour.

As much as it may militate against great-power conflict, globalization can also disrupt the international order in ways that actually increase the odds of war.

This paradox played out before WWI, when industrialization created enormous wealth whose uneven distribution simultaneously reordered societies and upset prevailing balances of power. Rising industrial giants like Germany aggressively pursued greater international influence, while rulers in Vienna and Istanbul struggled to keep their polyglot empires intact, and entrenched elites everywhere stoked nationalism to distract an increasingly restive proletariat. By upending traditional social and political arrangements, this previous period of globalization unleashed centrifugal forces that ultimately tore apart the old order.

A century later, globalization has again created winners and losers, both within and between nations. In the United States and Europe, populist politicians increasingly scapegoat immigrants and minorities, bankers and trading partners, and the very institutions that for generations heralded democratic progress and economic prosperity. China, which has profited handsomely within this established world order, now plays the part of spoiler seeking a larger slice of the geopolitical pie, while Russia's leaders do what they can to exacerbate anti-establishment tendencies for their own short-term benefit.

Globalization has indeed made much of the world so economically interdependent that it renders war objectively unprofitable—yet it has also sown the seeds of potential future conflicts. Whether the great illusion of war will again deceive political leaders in the 21st century depends in large part on how effectively national governments and international institutions resolve the inherent contradictions of modern capitalism, and continue to leverage the more peaceful logic of mutual economic benefit.

Can international institutions constrain great-power conflict?

Since at least the time of Thucydides, realism has dominated the study of international relations, explaining the propensity for great-power conflict in terms of human nature and systemic anarchy. But what accounts for cooperation among states? Liberalism emerged from the Enlightenment as a competing school of thought, emphasizing the importance of international institutions, free trade, and the spread of democracy in mitigating conflict—and positing a theory of change promising a more peaceful future.

For all the talk of anarchy in international relations, states do tend to cooperate on a myriad of issues. Unlike the classic "prisoner's dilemma" that rewards defection, states have to live with the lasting consequences of their iterative foreign policy choices, making mutual cooperation an eminently rational choice. As their interests converge in a given area, states routinely enter into arrangements with one another, from informal consultations to binding treaties and international organizations, that more efficiently and productively manage their interactions. In practice, such cooperative regimes produce far more "win-win" outcomes than zero-sum solutions.

The 1648 Peace of Westphalia, which famously introduced the modern concept of state sovereignty, also inaugurated the use of multinational gatherings to resolve international disputes. Such ad hoc conferences became a recurring feature of European diplomacy following the 1815 Congress of Vienna—which also established the world's first intergovernmental organization, to manage navigation on the Rhine—and it wasn't long before international conventions in Geneva and The Hague began codifying laws of war.

Founded following World War I, the League of Nations was the first international organization focused on maintaining world peace, and it failed miserably owing in part to poor institutional design and lack of U.S. membership. However, this idealistic experiment paved the way for the United Nations, which has successfully resolved numerous conflicts since the Second World War through diplomacy, economic sanctions, peacekeeping operations, and even the use of military force. Nowadays, most countries insist on UN Security Council authorization before going to war, and even the great powers pay lip service to this influential institution as a forum for registering their foreign policy positions.

Beyond the UN, the United States championed a variety of multilateral regimes to promote global economic growth and regional integration in the wake of World War II, including the International Monetary Fund, World Trade Organization, NATO military alliance, and the European Union. These institutions not coincidentally served as bulwarks against Soviet expansion during the Cold War, and were instrumental in the transition of Eastern Europe to "Western" democracy and capitalism after the collapse of the USSR. They have unquestionably contributed to making Europe whole, free, and at peace.

Regional integration has been much less successful in Asia, however, where U.S. influence has been exercised primarily through bilateral arrangements among mutually mistrustful partners that only recently began to fear a rising China. Since taking up its UNSC seat in 1971, Beijing has proven itself more adept than Moscow at playing well with others in multilateral forums, joining Asia-Pacific Economic Cooperation and the WTO before its northern neighbour and establishing the Asian Infrastructure Investment Bank as a potential rival to the World Bank and IMF. With the launch of its massive Belt and Road Initiative and the U.S. withdrawal from the Trans-Pacific Partnership, China is institutionalizing its regional hegemony—and challenging U.S. leadership—in ways Russia must envy.

While the proliferation of cooperative international regimes has certainly bound most states together in ways that makes war among them less likely, it puts far fewer constraints on the great powers, who jealously guard their privileged positions atop the international system. Beijing rejected arbitration under the UN Convention on the Law of the Sea over its South China Sea claims; Moscow annexed Crimea in contravention of the Budapest Memorandum on Security Assurances; and Washington routinely engages in bombing campaigns with the flimsiest of legal pretexts.

Moreover, the future of international cooperation seems increasingly uncertain. The current American president disdains the very multilateralism that for generations enhanced U.S. power and prosperity; China is promoting alternative arrangements that promise far less transparency and accountability; and Russia is intent on undermining NATO and the EU at any cost. The less committed these great powers become to prevailing security regimes, the more likely they are to disregard longstanding norms of international cooperation and multilateral conflict resolution—which could be a very dangerous development, indeed.

Ultimately, international institutions can constrain conflict—but only insofar as the great powers play along. And for Beijing, Moscow, and Washington, it's an anarchic world after all.

Can the world be made safe through democracy?

From a realist perspective, international relations amounts to little more than a power struggle among states, each of which acts essentially the same, regardless of its particular nature. Like billiard balls ricocheting off one another in an anarchic game of realpolitik, states amount to "black boxes" whose external behaviour reveals nothing about their internal workings—or so the theory goes. But a growing body of empirical evidence suggests democracies can behave quite differently than other states, with profound implications for the future of warfare.

The Enlightenment philosopher Immanuel Kant was first to recognize that a world of constitutional republics might someday bring perpetual peace, but it wasn't until the 20th century that liberal democracy became widespread enough to put his hypothesis to the test. Since then, study after study has found that wars between mature democracies are indeed less common than conflicts involving other kinds of states. Kant anticipated this phenomenon would come about because citizens who bear the human and financial costs of war would naturally be cautious if empowered to authorize hostilities. Furthermore, democratic political norms favouring compromise and respect for human rights tend to make republics a bit less bellicose—at least when dealing with states similarly governed.

This democratic peace theory comes with a caveat, however: When confronted by autocracies, democracies are just as likely to wage war as any other state. Aggressive imperialist, fascist, and communist regimes repeatedly learned this lesson during the 20th century, often finding that their democratic rivals could mobilize superior political and economic resources when provoked. On the other hand, autocratic regimes that transitioned to democracy—such as Germany and Japan following World War II— became much less threatening to their neighbours, as Kant's hypothesis predicted.

Given these developments, it's not surprising that the United States and its democratic allies came to view the promotion of democracy around the world as a matter of self-interest. Whether inspired by liberal ideals or neoconservative concerns, "making the world safe for democracy" became synonymous in many Western circles with making the world safe *through* democracy—that is, pressuring autocratic regimes to adopt democratic reforms, by force if necessary, for the sake of both national security and human rights. Sadly, American diplomatic and military efforts since 9/11 to spread democracy at gunpoint ended in disaster, arguably making the world less safe.

Compounding this trend is the troubling decline, after decades of almost uninterrupted progress, in the number of fully functioning democracies around the world. Illiberal regimes have come to power in Venezuela, Turkey, Hungary, and elsewhere around the world, and the erosion of democratic norms in the United States has undermined America's soft-power appeal and claims to leadership of the so-called "free world." Nevertheless, reports of democracy's death are greatly exaggerated; for all its flaws, the social, economic, and, yes, security benefits of this form of government still greatly outweigh any alternatives, and it is likely to further spread in the future.

Although democracy has undoubtedly reduced warfare among its practitioners, it is unlikely to diminish the potential for great-power conflict anytime soon. On the contrary, Western democracy-promotion efforts have exacerbated tensions with Moscow, which blames Washington for the "colour revolutions" that overthrew friendly regimes in Ukraine, Georgia, and across the Arab world, while Beijing is wary of any political liberalization that might undermine the Community Party's hold on power. Consequently, Russia and China have emerged as exemplars of authoritarian governance, undemocratic alternatives to the United States in a multipolar world. Meanwhile, America's emergence as a great power actually led to its war-making deliberations becoming less democratic. Congress has gradually ceded its constitutional authority over national security issues to the president, while the voting public has largely lost interest in military matters since the end of mass conscription and the advent of an all-volunteer force. Under such circumstances, great-power behavior can often bear a striking resemblance to billiard balls after all.

What if anarchy is merely what we make of it?

The international system has changed considerably since the appearance of the modern nation-state in the 17th century. Over time, more and more countries around the world have discovered the advantages of democratic governance, economic integration, and political cooperation in multilateral forums—and their interactions with each other have evolved as a consequence. Although anarchy continues to lurk behind the scenes, many actors on the international stage no longer seem bound by scripts of power politics or structural imperatives.

In recent decades, a new theory has emerged to explain this evolution. Constructivism asserts that international relations are not the immutable result of human nature or material structures, but instead are socially created through shared ideas. Alexander Wendt and other constructivist scholars contend that social interactions give meaning to ideas, which in turn shape the identities and interests of international actors—and it is these social constructions, not anarchy itself, that determine the nature of international relations. In other words, anarchy is what states make of it—and while some may respond with self-help schemes, others increasingly choose international cooperation and collective security.

If anarchy really is what states make of it, then their changing worldviews ought to have some effect on international relations. There are many schools of thought as to what drives such social change, but one of the more intriguing was advanced by Ken Wilber as a "theory of everything." Building on the "spiral dynamics" model of human development first formulated by Clare Graves, Wilber contends that individuals pass through discrete developmental stages—from egocentric to ethnocentric to "world centric" and potentially beyond—as they mature, contributing to the aggregate mix of developmental levels present in the larger society. If enough people within a society begin exhibiting emerging levels of consciousness, its developmental "centre of gravity" may shift toward this higher-order worldview.

The impact of such social evolution on international relations could be profound. Referring to developmental levels as color-coded "memes," Wilber suggested that societies where an ethnocentric worldview ("blue" meme) prevails would likely see others as threats, while those at the next higher level ("orange" meme), embracing autonomy and scientific materialism, might treat them as competitors. Among those societies in Europe and North America where a pluralistic, postmodern "green" meme is more pronounced, international cooperation has become the norm. However, upward progress is not inevitable; even in "advanced" Western societies, approximately 70 percent of the population remains at the "blue" level or below, making regression to previous levels of development an ever-present possibility.

The corollary of shared ideas shaping international relations is that not everyone is always reading from the same script. States where the "green" meme is manifest still have to deal with countries operating at the "orange" and "blue" levels—not to mention the occasional power-hungry, egocentric "red" regime. Put another way, while liberal democracies like the United States and its allies traditionally see international relations in cooperative, "win-win" terms, states whose worldviews centre around competition and conflict cannot be easily ignored.

Unfortunately, until all the great powers embrace a more cooperative, less confrontational vision of international relations, war among them remains a real possibility. There are few signs that Chinese or Russian societies are developing in this direction—or that their autocratic political systems would respond well to such social change. Meanwhile, U.S. advocacy for the liberal world order it helped create has become lukewarm in recent years, while less lofty ethnocentric and authoritarian sentiments are making a comeback across the globe, threatening to drag a number of nations back down the proverbial development spiral.

Even if we suppose that further progress in international relations is simply a matter of shared belief, getting all the great powers to imagine anarchy in the same way is no simple matter. And until they each construct worldviews centred on international cooperation and mutual interests, conflict among them is far easier to envision.

Is the United States still indispensable?

"We are the indispensable nation. We stand tall and we see further than other countries into the future, and we see the danger here to all of us."

— Madeleine Albright

International relations have changed substantially in the century since the First World War—and especially after its sequel ended some seven decades ago. Competition between half a dozen or so great powers boiled down to two, then just one as the Cold War culminated in American hegemony. Far from the end of history, however, this unipolar moment naturally proved unsustainable, and China, Russia, and even some U.S. allies soon began reasserting themselves on the international stage. Should this proliferation of great powers be a cause for concern?

Probably. A consensus has emerged in recent years among international security experts that the potential for great-power conflict is increasing. The 2018 U.S. National Defence Strategy declared the re-emergence of long-term, strategic competition by revisionist powers as the central challenge to U.S. prosperity and security, superseding terrorism as the principal threat. In 2016, the National Intelligence Council identified the changing nature of conflict as a global trend with key implications, forecasting that the risk of conflict will increase through 2035 in part due to diverging interests among the major powers. The World Economic Forum reached a similar conclusion in 2016, warning that a major conventional conflict between great powers was possible by 2030.

The reasons for these concerns are obvious. During the Cold War, the United States established a persistent security presence in regions once dominated by China, then expanded the NATO alliance right up to Russia's borders following the collapse of the Soviet Union, setting each of these regional hegemons up for conflict as they began reasserting power within their traditional spheres of influence. Unlike former U.S. adversaries such as Germany and Japan, who learned to play well with others after embracing democracy several generations ago, China and Russia remain ruled by authoritarian regimes intent on challenging U.S. global leadership. And they are each developing high-end military capabilities designed to neutralize American strengths and project force beyond their borders, shifting the balance of power in much of Europe and Asia. A U.S. congressional commission recently warned that the United States might struggle to win—or perhaps lose—a war against China or Russia.

Still, there is cause for hope. Since the end of the last world war, the United Nations and various regional security institutions have provided useful venues for great powers to address their differences, with international law and shifting social norms gradually marginalizing war as an acceptable dispute-resolution mechanism. Globalization of trade and investment has undoubtedly lowered the risk of war between the

United States and China, while Russia has seemingly adopted a strategy of indirect action—competition short of armed conflict—in its interactions with America and its allies. And so long as each great power maintains a credible nuclear deterrent, the promise of mutually assured destruction should continue to temper escalatory impulses.

Even though the risk of great-power conflict is rising, there is nothing inevitable about this outcome. Neither China nor Russia is spoiling for a fight with the U.S. military, which is likely to maintain superiority over each adversary through at least the middle of the century. Although anti-American sentiment has drawn Beijing and Moscow closer together in recent years, it is doubtful they will overcome longstanding mutual suspicions to join forces against the United States anytime soon. However, America could easily be drawn into conflicts between these great powers and U.S. allies such as Taiwan or the Baltic states—presuming, of course, that the U.S. government remains committed to defending its most vulnerable partners.

The future of great-power conflict, then, is largely a function of U.S. foreign policy. As a superpower in relative decline, the United States has neither the economic wherewithal nor political will to prevent China and Russia from assuming more prominent roles on the international stage. Washington must now give serious consideration as to which aspects of the liberal world order and its network of alliances—which it built and sustained for the better part of a century— remain vital to U.S. national security an era of renewed great-power competition.

For example, NATO continues to provide obvious security benefits to the United States—including neutralizing the European Union as a potential great-power rival—but it makes little sense to extend alliance membership to former Soviet states like Georgia or Ukraine while Moscow retains the capability and intent to dominate its "near abroad." Similarly, it's only a matter of time before Beijing can conquer Taipei while degrading a U.S. military response, which means finding a peaceful solution to the "One China" problem is imperative if America hopes to escape the "Thucydides trap" that has accompanied rising powers for millennia.

Yet even if the United States pursues a realist foreign policy approach to China and Russia, it must nevertheless remain true to the liberal principles that underpin its prosperity and global influence. America cannot afford to abandon its steadfast support for democracy, free trade, and the rule of law in favour of isolationism or an "America first" approach that befuddles allies and emboldens enemies. Few other great powers have ever wielded the sort of moral authority and soft-power appeal that the United States enjoyed until recently—and no other nation can claim to be quite so indispensable to world peace.

Craig Perry

Decision Making For A Regenerative Society

1. Futuring cultural dynamics

2. Rethinking societal organization

3. Rebalancing societal governance

4. Civic engagement futures

5. Societal artificial constructs of tomorrow

6. Literacy for year 20018

7. Rewriting freedom of speech

8. Trust beyond the present

9. Thank you for eating

10. Sketching the unthinkable

11. Artificial intelligence and us

12. Do you wonder how to ignite futures for a regenerative society?

Futuring cultural dynamics

Most policy decision-making models are based on demographic information that considers elements such as sex or ethnicity, as the staples of diversity. They aim to tell the story of particular population segments. However, over the last few decades, globalization and significant political shifts have driven substantial growth in population migration. From the turn of the century, the number of international migrants has increased by 70%.

The shift has boosted the stream of people's interactions, coupled with their actions, perceptions, impressions, observations, and interpretations, across time, space, and scale. Ethnographic and cultural heritage experts identify this fluid stream of change with culture. They would argue that migratory impacts are most likely to span decades.

The aftermath of increased migration seems to raise questions about how cultures might evolve. Traditional demographic methods have difficulties in identifying the nuanced metamorphosis of population segments. As a result, policy-making appears to miss critical cultural developments that would otherwise pinpoint characteristics and needs of populations in flux. By excluding cultural nuances in policy making, do we limit our choices for the future?

In *The Art of Choice*, Iyengar defines choice as "the ability to exercise control over ourselves and our environment. To choose, we must perceive that control is possible."

She argues that the type of culture we grew up in influences our understanding of what choices are available to us. For example, as children, each of us heard some expectations about our future. Some of us were told to *do what our family tells us to do,* or others might have been asked *what would you like to do?* The former might tend to look up at their elders to show the path in life and protect them from selecting the wrong choices. The latter might be better off when exercising the personal option. The two approaches associate with collectivistic and individualistic community types, respectively.

Individualism/collectivism is one of several other cultural dimensions. Cultural studies experts measured these dimensions at country-level. They believe that the scores are stable over time as they reflect values transferred from parents to children and rarely change in later life. The experts argue that our early-life exposure to these cultural dimensions has consequences on our formative and adult years and the relationship between our identities and how we choose.

Nevertheless, most recent migratory trends have usually involved younger generations. Between now and later life, newcomers adjust to their new location, live and go to school in a new cultural environment, while bringing forward their cultural heritage. During the transition, migrants' old and new cultures mingle. Traditional population segmentation methods cannot capture such transitional nuances. Existing policy-making tools do not seem to give justice to these individuals, and the societies they live in, anymore.

Cultural economists, data ethnographers, or those focused on culture analytics and social networks have also attempted to define and model cultural indicators. Their information-intensive approaches seem limited though in capturing culture's fluid states of emergence, transformation, limitation, disappearance, and renewal.

Should instruments aiming to capture the transition of cultures include, beyond cultural dimensions, elements such as societal structure (e.g., globalized vs.

distributed/local), population dynamics (e.g., participatory vs. siloed), intellectual humility (e.g., agility vs. consistency in holding opinions), resilience, or the nature-culture dualism?

Wouldn't decision-making and policy design be better informed by a lively cultural understanding mediated through both economic and ethnographic approaches that are constituents to one another, not separate of each other?

Rethinking societal organization

Today, emotions seem to run high about trade, politics, governments, policy, national pride, and much more. Numerous individuals may feel disenfranchised. How might society be organized such that it enables its members' agency to harmonize civic rights and responsibilities with their values and aspirations?

Society is an instinctive human organization in which individuals continuously interact with each other, making it a living entity. Its members might share a similar social fabric, or live in the same geographical area, or participate in the same political-economic-social governance structure and avenues for civic engagement.

The two fundamental concepts that society has structured itself into are nation and state. Being human-made, both ideas are artificial. A nation is a group of individuals who share a common heritage. A state is linked to a territory and its internationally-recognized boundaries. A nation-state is a nation living within a state. In many contexts, a nation-state is equivalent to a country.

These concepts were born in the mid-1600s, during the negotiations for the Peace of Westphalia. This treaty established the foundation for international law, diplomacy, sovereignty, foreign and internal affairs, which ended wars and empires, while recognizing multiple states, most being nation-states. Some might feel inclined to note that in a way, the treaty ended the times' flavour of globalization. At that time, nation would mostly live within the boundaries of a state. As such, the distance between nation and state was almost non-existent.

How has the 17th-century concept of the nation-state fared so far? After the Westphalian Treaty, it seems that the nation-state model had been increasingly successful in Europe, by which it was adopted in the colonies, and beyond. Due to its wide adoption, one could argue that this was the first global treaty in that it paved the way for the first globalisation in the 18th century.

Down the road, during post-colonialism, while borders were drawn sometimes artificially, nations might've been split amongst several states, introducing some distance between nation and state. Nevertheless, the Westphalian nation-state has continued to succeed, registering its peak during the peace treaties that ended World War I.

Since then though, the nation-state seems to have declined. In the aftermath of World War II, the artificial divide introduced by the Iron Curtain was (in historical terms) short-lived. Once the Curtain fell, everyone wanted to see what was outside of it. Furthermore, the development of the European Union eliminated the borders amongst some member states. It enables each nation to travel, work, and live without boundaries across the EU while preserving the autonomy and territory of its member states. In such an environment, state borders switched from an international to an internal, administrative affair. In this context, representatives of several nations could now live within the boundaries of one state. As such, the overlap between nation and state has diminished. Nations and states seem to have continued to grow further apart.

Similar migratory trends have been observed well beyond Europe. World political and economic tensions have pushed individuals to seek living solutions beyond their birth nation-state. As a result, migration is at an all-time high. A nation now has representation across multiple states. For example, the Indian diaspora spread across the world contributes not only to the development of their adopted country, but also to that of India. In the process, they also make their heritage known outside their country of birth, creating nuances of it elsewhere. The concepts of nation and state seem to have continued to grow further apart.

Migration seems to have changed the nation-state relationship in two ways. First, the relation between nation and state is not one-to-one anymore. Second, the two concepts don't overlap as they did during Westphalian times. A distance between them has been emerging.

What should happen with this growing distance, especially when considering the role of the nation-state in the politics-economics-social governance and in civic engagement? The situation could become even more complicated when considering how unpredictable extreme natural, political, or economic events might push populations to seek shelter in friendlier territories. Furthermore, with increasing signs of globalization shifting to more decentralized, local, but distributed preferences, trade and information wars, etc., one could wonder whether we are living the modern version of pre-Westphalia. What would it take to build a contemporary model addressing societal organization issues that becomes at least as successful as the one built in the 17th century?

Rebalancing societal governance

The two fundamental concepts that society has organized itself into are nation and state. The success of this model was observed when the distance between nation and state was almost non-existent. Today, the nation and state seem to have distanced considerably. Although society's organizational model has shifted, its governance structure still follows the one intended for the stage when nation and state almost overlapped.

The nation-state governs society's internal (e.g., law, tax) and external (e.g., defence) affairs through a governing entity structure based on three interacting systems: political, economic, and social. The three systems operate most successfully when they are in balance. The equilibrium between the societal economic and social systems is meant to be maintained by politics. Imagine this balance as a triangle with all three sides equal, with politics as its top vertex, and the economic and social dimensions as the other two vertices at the bottom. Imbalance arises when the three sides are not equal anymore. The situation arises created when one of the vertices overshadows the other two, or when two vertices grow apart. As an example, some might consider that the exacerbation of religion, during various time periods, elevated the importance and influence of the social system, at the expense of the economic and political ones.

Nowadays, it seems that politics' capability to balance economy and society has dwindled again. This time, economic dominance prevails. The economic vertex has outgrown the politics and social ones. With this, the distance between the political and social system has increased. As such, the two aspects left behind by the overgrown economic system (i.e., political and social), often struggle. What has changed since the days when societal governance operated optimally on a foundation of its balanced political, economic, social systems?

Exponential advancement in technology enables the world to connect globally, share information and collaborate in ways not possible before, further transforming the political, economic, and social systems. Big data and social networks have created powerful feedback loops between information and political micro targeting, partisanship, and polarization. Ironically, such tactics have diminished ideological differentiation amongst political parties, while strengthening party unity in decision-making for those elected to serve in governing bodies. In the process, partisans are incentivized to participate in the voting process, while the rest are forgotten, increasing their disengagement in politics. The question is how could the use of big data and social networks be turned around to take us back to what democratic politics used to be?

Economic dominance and technology seem to have increased the level of collaboration amongst groups of nation-states and their citizens, enabling migration. Migrants participate right away in the economic and social system of their new country. They engage in the development of their new country through economic and social contributions, yet have little say in the democratic process. Obtaining the right to vote and participating in politics has a lengthy time lag, which excludes them from political engagement. As a result, societal governance tends to misrepresent their rights and responsibilities. The political-economic-social is, once more, unbalanced.

In the process, the nation-state has diminished its capacity to ensure the protection, development, and well-being of its citizens through edifices such as education, healthcare, or culture. Given the increasing distance between nation and state, and the imbalance observed in the political-economic-social governance, how might a society organize and govern itself such that its citizens feel empowered to harmonize civic rights and responsibilities with their values and aspirations?

Civic engagement futures

Society is an instinctive human structure. Society established the concepts of nation and state to *organize* itself. It developed the political, economic, and social systems to *govern* itself. It created the notions of citizenship and residency to *engage* its people.

Citizenship establishes rights and responsibilities linked to a country, its democratic and governance systems, and borders. The status can be acquired either at birth, based on the parent's citizenship and/or the territory of birth, or later, through naturalization in a foreign land. Residency refers to the physical location where a person lives. It provides a framework to exercise rights and responsibilities related to daily life, such as earning a living or education. Citizenship seems linked to the concept of nation and democratic participation in politics, whereas residency connects with economics and social matters, and the notion of state.

Citizenship dates to ancient Greece. A citizen was someone who was born and lived in a city, having rights and responsibilities linked to both the organization and governance of that city. As such, at that time, citizenship and residency overlapped. Similarly, following the Peace of Westphalia, when an individual was very likely to be a member of one nation living within the borders of one state, the citizenship and residency coincided.

Nowadays, world citizens traveling, working, and living in jurisdictions different than those of their place of birth, embrace multiple citizenships. At the other end of the scale are those who have either lost all privilege or renounced their citizenship in protest of losing trust in the system. Civic engagement allows an individual to have from one to multiple residencies and from none to many citizenships.

Citizenship has become virtually borderless in the European Union (EU), which is an international body of collaboration. In this context, citizenship now represents mostly an individual's national origin, together with their participation in the democratic process in their country of origin. Residency links individual's rights and responsibilities with the territory in which they earn money and access systems that support their daily life.

The concept of residency is then kicked up a notch by one of EU's members, Estonia. In its quest for competitive advantage, the country has become a leader in digital governance. Estonia has branded itself as the "new digital nation for global citizens" through its e-residency program. Estonian e-residency is an online platform that enables anyone in the world to register a business and manage its money. For example, it provides access to a network of financial and other professional services. An applicant becomes an Estonian e-resident and receives a government-issued digital identification, based on government identification from their country of origin. In this context, e-residency raises questions about how the digital government manages one's foreign credentials, and how the entrepreneur governs its business legally across borders.

Concurrently, e-residency seems to be a flavour of investor citizenship, offered by many other countries that aim to attract capital, for which, in turn, they provide an expedited path to citizenship. In the process, the concept of citizenship has shifted even more towards economics, losing its flair for political debate and democracy.

The Chinese social credit score has piloted another alternative to civic engagement. The program aggregates an individual's political, economic, and social data. A high score gives priority access to higher flexibility and living standards such as career advancement, housing, or mobility. The system takes the Western versions of the marketplace and social media aggregation to a new level of profiling, social value, and societal stratification. The social credit score seems to considerably amplify the social and economic aspects while keeping an eye on political activities. Such a paradigm raises significant ethical and moral questions, questioning one's ability to exercise civic rights and responsibilities regardless of the score.

Such emerging types of civic engagement seem to play at the intersection of several dimensions: (1) links to the physical place(s) of birth, work, or living; (2) the omnipresence of daily life; and (3) levels of trust in the societal organization, governance, and engagement.

At the same time, the concepts of citizenship and residency do not overlap as they once did. In the process, civic engagement seems to struggle with who and where one can vote so that they can have a say in the democratic process. For example, some migrants can still vote in their country of birth. Although they have lived abroad for a long time, losing touch with the realities of that state, their civic engagement influences decisions for the daily life of those who remained. Is it fair to those who stayed? Concurrently, migrants cannot vote in the country of their residency, where they are not yet citizens, although they contribute to the economic and social system. Is it fair to these newcomers?

As society continues its fluid advancement, should it consider transferring citizenship rights and responsibilities to the concept of residency related to the territory surrounding our everyday life, rather than the place of birth?

Societal artificial constructs of tomorrow

Society's means to organize, govern, and civically engage are artificial constructs. They interact with each other and with the intuitive, non-artificial aspects of society. As one would expect, the interactions are in continuous motion. Consequently, over long stretches of time, the distances amongst societal constructs have varied. However, history has shown several moments in time when such distances and interactions functioned at an optimal level. Could those moments inspire our look into societal futures and the ability to act towards a preferred vision?

Society's means of organization, the nation-state and its links to international law and diplomacy, were established in 1648 by the European Peace of Westphalia. The treaty brought peace and equality amongst nations, the states they lived in, and religions they practiced, ending centuries-old fights and empires. It defined the role and responsibilities of a state, its relation to the nation(s) on its territory, and other states. At the time the model registered such great success, the concepts of nation and state almost overlapped. The distance between them was minimal.

Society's means of governance, the political-economic-social system, is optimal when politics balance the economic and social components, maintaining the similar size of and distances amongst the three.

Society's engagement model relies on the concepts of citizenship and residency. Citizenship seems to be closely linked to that of the nation, since most individuals would acquire it at birth, based on their parents' citizenship. In this sense, citizenship is also closely linked to one's ethnicity. At the same time, residency seems to link more with the administrative functions related to territory and performed by the state. In a nation-state, citizenship and residency would be identical most of the times. The distance between them would be minimal. At the same time, citizenship seems to be the tool to participate in a nation's politics as one would require that nation's passport to vote and participate in its democratic system. Residency is the tool to exercise one's rights and responsibilities related to the economy and society of that state.

History describes stories of flourishing periods. One could notice that some registered minimum distances amongst its artificial societal constructs. For example, during the golden age of ancient Greek civilization, in city-states, the concepts of nation and state, and those of citizenship and residency overlapped. During Westphalian times, the distance between nation and state, citizenship and residency, and politics, on one side, and economics and society was almost non-existent. What both these periods seem to have in common is that they operated in a network of entities that valued more local administration, e.g., the city-state, rather than the broader environment.

Over the last century or so, economic dominance, migration trends, and technological evolution seem to have contributed to the decline of the nation-state, society's way of organization. The political-economic-social balance in societal governance has also been affected. Such decline and imbalance have created confusion between the meaning of societal civic engagement, i.e., citizenship and residency. Considering the global trend toward urbanization, should society's artificial constructs be rooted in city-level everyday life, across networks of similar environments? What would it take for urban residents to be citizens too?

Their rights and responsibilities would straddle democratic political-economic-social participation within the boundaries of their city-level everyday life. The city would resemble a state. What would be different from past flourishing periods is that not one, but multiple nations would live in this state, as it already is the case in large urban areas. Such a model would take us back to society's non-artificial, intuitive, and fluid transitions and interactions of cultures and the questions raised by such dynamics.

Literacy for year 20018

At its origin, the term "literacy" meant *"the ability to read and write."* Although it was first recorded in the 19th century, coinciding with the beginning of the industrial era, specialists have studied its evolution starting from much earlier times. One of the ways they have tracked literacy was through signatures on marriage certificates. When discussing literacy and the industrial revolution, economic historians such as E.G. West, note that *"the evidence on literacy and schooling is interdependent."* His study suggests that *"literacy specialists usually describe figures of schooling as 'indirect evidence' of literacy. Schooling specialists, meanwhile, regard literacy as 'indirect evidence' of schooling."*

With the transition from the Industrial to the knowledge era, the term has evolved to convey the message of *"competence or knowledge in a specific area."* For example, in addition to reading and writing, organizations such as OECD discuss numeracy and financial literacy. Futurists advocate for future literacy. Others address health or science literacy, with reading and writing is now considered fundamental literacies.

What does it mean for the era we are in? Arguably, we are still attempting to understand what that is. The knowledge era seemed to have been first identified by Peter Drucker, in 1959, when he introduced the concept of the knowledge worker. Today, the term seems more relevant as ever. Some suggest that 2018 belongs to the era of the humans or the Anthropocene, while the World Economic Forum points to the fourth industrial revolution. Eras, nevertheless, seem to be better defined after the fact. Literacies, however, seem to prepare us for what's to come. Asking what these literacies are, regardless of how we choose to name an era, seems timely. Today's literacy types include technological and informational competencies, which have been essential for a while now. Such a trend appears to continue, but for how long could it last? With the current aims of developing systems that are highly usable by humans, will there continue to be a need for deep technological literacy?

What might the literacies for tomorrow look like? Would they still be interdependent with schooling, as noted for the industrial era? How could one prepare for a future when the current rate of change is high already?

While possible but unknown tomorrows unfold in our imagination, they still have two things in common: (1) they are uncertain; and (2) preparing for them is ambiguous. At the same time, most of us have difficulties dealing with ambiguity. In fact, social psychologist Geert Hofstede has identified "*uncertainty avoidance*" as one of the six dimensions of culture. His study across about 100 nations, reveals that globally, the human comfort with ambiguity sits, on average, at about 36%. The other 64% of the time, humans seem to prefer to control the future. The higher such preference is, the more rigid the codes of beliefs, behaviour, and intolerance are.

But how could one control the future? At best, we can prepare. Getting ready for next year seems attainable with current competencies. Bracing for five years from now would include a multitude of assumptions, and potentially competency changes. How about ten years out? Or fifty? The longer the time horizon, the more we seem to joke about and care less how far ahead we talk about. At the same time, such a view would encourage us to switch our thinking beyond what we know today.

In this context, let's say, the year is 20018, eighteen thousand years ahead of now. What literacies would prepare us for 20018? By that time, we could be back to an agrarian era, or become Martians, or non-existent altogether. Who knows? Breathing might become the literacy of those times. What would prepare us for such eras, seems to be our ability to deal with the ambiguity awaiting us. Shouldn't we think about ambiguity as critical literacy? How might such literacy be developed?

Some might argue that ambiguity develops during critical thinking or resilience practice or training events. The same event though still sets the expectations for a determined outcome by the end of it, such as earning a grade, job, or advancement. Others might point to life events or religion as good teachers of ambiguity.

Overall, the current schooling system cannot train us to be at ease in ambiguous environments. So do most of existing societal dimensions, including economics, politics, and governance. Isn't it the time to address that?

Rewriting freedom of speech

Many can only dream of having the freedom to express their opinion. The fortunate of us might take it for granted. Others might see it through biased lenses. I acknowledge mine, originating from growing up in a former communist country. In that world, information dissemination meant precisely two hours of evening TV programming. Any form of expression linked everything back to the doctrine regurgitating "glorious" dictatorship propaganda. Information beyond meant treason. Asking for a passport just to explore a different culture, stamped one as being against the system. Censorship was deeply entrenched in everyday life. It should come as no surprise that the world after the cold war sought freedom of access and expression.

But with little knowledge on how to achieve that after 50 years of communist rule. As a result, even today, after almost another 30 years, the discovery of free speech is continuing. Experimentation with extreme polarization is allowed. Perhaps unknowingly, essential aspects of freedom, well-being, or even human rights are impacted. Foul language, objectifying those who are different, or talk shows exploiting fear are such examples.

However, everywhere else the discovery of what free speech may become seems to also be in question. The internet has opened massive channels of online communication. It has increased our acceptance of sharing more about ourselves, even intertwining our private and public selves. To stay informed, and to speak up when we see fit, we use a multitude of devices and apps. We freely give our consent to provide pieces of our private information. More recently though, the online life that we thought was public, has increasingly become an island that we inhabit together with those like us. The software is becoming more and more sophisticated, learning about our preferences and presenting us with the information it thinks we want. In the process it isolates us in our own world. Not realizing we live with a different flavour of privacy, we still stay always online, expecting everything to happen now, while disseminating instantly what resonates with us, thus reinforcing the attributes of the data silo forming our world.

The paradox of the bubble is that it still drives the fragmentation of our attention with methods that have their own chapters in economics, politics, or social realms. Some are fair, some are not. Most of these methods have recently emerged and our language is catching up with the times by adding these contemporary meanings to the dictionary. For example, "someone who posts inflammatory messages online to provoke emotional responses" is called an internet troll. Sadly, though, our "always on," instant, share-all expectations have become a medium for expanding trolling into the physical world, making it ubiquitous. With this, everything goes, it seems, including extreme, hateful, and harmful speech that has been recently coined in media as the "weaponization" of free speech.

We have the freedom *of* assembly, religion, and speech, or the freedom *to* marry and love, but is this enough? OCAD Professor Suzanne Stein argues for a "greater form of freedom: freedom *from* harm."

The question is what do we do about it? Perhaps zooming into this proliferation of trolling, online anonymity, social media bubbles and their connection with the fight for our attention would provide an answer. In a world in which we've become omnipresent, attention fragmentation seems to illustrate the contemporary version of the divide and conquer paradigm. Attention holds the key to today's competitive advantage, starting from the individual level. At the same time, the more we realize our attention is selective yet limited, the more we seem to crave it while giving it freely away at the expense of freedom itself. Has the freedom *for* attention become a basic need, and right?

Trust beyond the present

Trust is a social construct essential to economic and societal development. However, trust has issues that the passing of time has not only not yet solved but also blurred any futures orientation. Furthermore, while technology presents possible solutions, it also introduces new challenges. One would expect that science has resolved such issues, but science itself has undergone a trust crisis. A solution to re-establishing trust is designing the future with the society itself.

In 2017, trust in official institutions registered a collapse in the US and a significant drop in the UK, after a steady decline over time. Decades earlier, behind the Iron Curtain, the communist regime thrived through the propagation of mistrust.

Centuries ago, the victory or defeat in war was a question of how the communication amongst generals, stationed at various locations, was transmitted through trusted, non-forgeable links. The system, at that time, did not have any control or feedback loop to ensure traitors did not intercept and interfere with the message. Dubbed the Byzantine Generals' problem in mathematics, in many ways similar to the Prisoners' Dilemma in economics, the challenge might now be solved by blockchain technology, with its promise for a single record of fact between two parties involved in a transaction.

Even if blockchain succeeds, another technology facet raises trust questions: data. With staggering amounts of data available but a remarkably low percentage analyzed, and even smaller amounts validated, how do we know whether we can count on the truth of this content?

The belief that scientific research is a trusted leader is also challenged. Investigations show that less than 50% of psychology studies could be replicated, together with increasing instances of corruption, including priming effects, fake peer reviews, or proliferation of citation cartels.

Extending the question of trust to forward-looking settings enhances decision makers' ability to anticipate possible futures and navigate risks and uncertainties, especially when trust moulds into "the willingness to be vulnerable to another party's actions." Trust in futures thinking enhances the capacity to embrace opportunities presented by "actionable images of the future" while deflecting weaknesses and threats.

A solution to re-establishing trust is expanding its definition from being an ingredient that catalyses economic prosperity and social life for people, to envisioning futures of a society with people. This participatory approach is diametrically opposed to the communist doctrine as well as the hierarchical, patriarchal, belief, and value systems that underlie existing power structures. Participation not only increases the likelihood of trusting what could be developed but also the engagement to ignite futures and shape the preferred one.

The reciprocal relationship between participation and trust is self-explanatory: participation spawns trust through dialogue, transparency, and agency, while trusting beliefs and actions (e.g., ability, benevolence, integrity) strengthen participation through the willingness to engage, take action, and break various barriers such as personal, situational, functional, or psychological.

Such relationship alleviates the anxiety of unknown futures through mental training and careful orchestration of expert and participant involvement. For example, while futurists' skill is critical in trend analysis to unearth blind spots and set the stage for grounded results, diversity and wide participation is more beneficial than competence during the next phase focused on opportunity prioritization. Further refining of selected opportunities is easily enabled by experimental prototyping of actionable future narratives, as a method to understand and handle the uncertainties and risks of unproven ideas about the future. The experts' facilitation skills and toolkits, such as empathy maps, role-playing, or installations, contribute to establishing the need, desire, and feasibility of building the envisioned futures.

As a final note, participation to build trust is the opportunity to develop further the networked society in which the collaboration amongst creativity, ethnographic, foresight, and analytical approaches convert the unknown into a viable and promising future for society.

Thank you for eating

Unless a major pandemic, war, or other disaster happens, the world population is projected to grow from about 7.5 billion today to a number in the range of 10 billion by 2050.

How would such growth be possible when, even today, there are large regions in the world struggling to provide basic needs, such as food to its population? This significant question is not only on the minds of many but also a strong focus for many organizations.

As a result of the abundant discussions, approaches, and actions, food has become a substantial political issue and one that is interconnected with multiple other even more significant debates. Major disputes that come to mind relate to the environment (e.g., habitat loss, soil degradation) and climate change. Resource (e.g., water, land) usage and rights are equally important. More complications are brought onboard by international development, global trade, health epidemics, and societal problems (e.g., access to basic food, poverty, education and literacy, rising middle class in developing nations and their changes in taste and consumption). Last but not least, corporate interests, food lobbies, and technocracies also add to the list of significant debates related to food.

It comes as no surprise that such a complex and disjointed food system is profoundly struggling. Estimates indicate that the global society wastes 24% of the food produced for human consumption, 28% of people overeat, whilst 28% of individuals are malnourished.

Those who can afford try to take the problem in their own hands by embracing various movements, from eating local, to following a specific diet, such as paleo or gluten-free, to being preoccupied with ingredients and nutrient factors, amongst others. And then there are the "foodies" with appetites for sophisticated ingredients, food designs, experiences, and entertainment.

On the other hand, those who can't, scramble to find affordable options, which, many times comes in the form of fried, processed, loaded with salt and sugar food, thus continuously increasing health and other societal issues. How to tackle them?

Futurists imagine what food nutrients, gardens, and farms might look like several decades out. Activists have started talking about the Big Food, as an analogy to Big Tobacco. This is no a coincidence at all. After all, paraphrasing Hippocrates, food is medicine. Similar to how tobacco has generated severe health conditions, so does the current corporate and industrial food paradigm.

Consistent and persistent anti-smoking national policies have been hugely successful in North America, where the smoking rate is at an all-time low. How did we get there? As WHO points out, there are six measures responsible for the progress: *"(1) monitor tobacco use and prevention policies; (2) protect people from tobacco use; (3) offer help to quit tobacco; (4) warn about the dangers of tobacco: (5) enforce bans on tobacco advertising, promotion, and sponsorship; (6)*

raise taxes on tobacco." These measures have been implemented over several decades, resulting in the decline in smoking rates in adults from over 40% to about 15%. Can we imagine what a similar reduction in diet-related diseases (e.g., obesity, heart disease, diabetes) would mean if similar food policies were implemented?

For countries like Norway, such imagination might already be a reality because of its recent introduction of a hefty tax on all sugary drinks, sweets and chocolate, chewing gum, and sweet biscuits. Other nations, such as France or UK have taken a more timid approach by taxing only sugary/sweetened drinks. As a result, even Norwegians might still be able to satisfy their sweet tooth just by crossing the border.

In the meantime, when health gets personal, it hits you head-on and might change habits much faster. It has worked for many people. It certainly has worked for me in fighting cancer. It was two years ago, ironically, in the middle of an advanced Futures class when my own future was in question. While it looks like I've beaten it so far, I credit this victory to a radical change in my approach to eating and drinking. It includes not only what, but when, how, and at what temperature, and learning how my body produces probiotics (and why they're important), and exchanges energy with the environment. I also learned how little food I need if I get the essential nutrients. As a result, I am now exploring how I might grow what I eat indoors. As a starter, it looks like even some veggies such as brussels sprouts are quite easy to grow. Sugar is not.

So, would a world void of sugar be possible? Furthermore, would a world in which the only food available is the one we grow at home be possible? How might that look like?

Sketching the unthinkable

In private and public administration, preparing for the future by "thinking the unthinkable" was first introduced by the RAND Corporation in the early 1960s. With time, sketching the unthinkable has become a common futuristic practice. Its results are summarized in stories about tomorrow, or scenarios.

And yet, scenarios are as old as humanity. Ancient civilizations imagined them in oracles or magic while building scenarios for the military (e.g., Sun Tzu's Art of War), describing both present traditions and future visions, especially during uncertain times. Scenarios are fundamental in military, policy, and business, being developed using a mix of disciplines such as mathematics, economics, anthropology, and story-telling.

Futurists Bishop and Kahane remind us about the three critical types of scenarios: (1) predictive, i.e., forecasts and what-ifs, asking "what *will* happen?"; (2) explorative, i.e., external and strategic, asking "what *can* happen?"; and (3) normative, e.g., preserving and transforming, asking "what *should* happen?".

The most known and used scenarios seem to fall into the first category. They are mostly based on statistics and assume they are bulletproof, based on scientists' never-ending proof of the "unreasonable effectiveness of mathematics." Nevertheless, when applied without checking the underlying nature of the relationships amongst the model's variables, predictions provide a false sense of security about futures. Time series are particularly prone to mistakes, as they might carry over underlying presumptions from past and present into futures, challenging the statistical condition for independence when extrapolating from one value to the next.

All three types of scenarios tell stories about possible futures, paving the path for envisioning adaptive strategies, but only normative scenarios expand the futures paradigm from predicting or thinking to practical actions that have the potential to shape the future.

The normative scenarios seem to be the least used. They initiated out of challenges brought on by significant shifts, such as a political regime change. In recent years, disciplines that promote open creativity, collaboration, and innovation have increasingly embraced normative scenarios.

Design-led disciplines such as design thinking, strategic design, or research through design bring to scenario development effective new methods such as visualization, aesthetics, ethnography, or experience design. They have taken the telling of a story to showing, feeling, and experiencing it. Such immersion creates that magical circle of trust around scenarios that gives leaders the confidence to embark on a hero's journey to act now and create "what *should* happen."

Nonetheless, design, futurism, and scientific methods for scenario development can further benefit from learning about each other.

For example, design's approach falls somewhere in between a binary selection (e.g., optimistic/pessimistic) and a high-medium-low style (e.g., most to least likely) which, most of the times, leads either to an optimistic-only path or, as the game theory demonstrates, to a sensible middle of the road but mediocre outcome. Futurism, on the other side, advocates for multiple, alternative futures that might have unpleasant or unexpected outcomes. At the same time, scientists look for theories that can provide evidence for the stories foresight scenarios aim to portray.

Could experiencing scenarios and the quest for hard facts be ever reconciled? Where might scenarios go from here? Would the futurists of 20018 still develop foresight scenarios? What would their toolset be?

In more immediate futures, data and ways to consume them are increasingly making their way into scenario development. Data have become essential in providing evidence of emerging blips that could turn into disruptors. Although digital and visual storytelling based on these data has progressed, the human brain, functioning in a 3-dimensional environment, still has difficulty making sense of large amounts of data presented on 2-dimensional screens.

These days it seems possible to narrow the gap between the 2-sided digital and the 3-dimensional physical worlds through augmented reality. This new technology enhances humans' ability to make sense of data by juxtaposing digital information onto the real world. Furthermore, as humans process information through their five senses, the visualization side of augmented reality could be paired up with sound, touch, scent, and even taste to portray the envisioned images of the future.

It is up to us now to test whether scenarios born out of signals, sifted through the growing universe of data, and felt through augmented reality experiences, can be more potent than existing scenario consumption methods. Can these envisioned stories generate action, agency, and resilience for building preferred futures?

Artificial intelligence and us

"Will AI take over the world?" is a common question across many news outlets these days. *"Artificial Intelligence will best humans at everything by 2060, experts say,"* predicts one of them. *"More than 70% of*

US fears robots taking over our lives, survey finds," describes another. Most of all, *"how long will it take for your job to be automated?"* seems to be the question on everyone's mind. Opposing views are also present, arguing about *"The great tech panic: robots won't take all our jobs."* How do we reconcile these views into what Artificial Intelligence is and can be?

The term *"Artificial Intelligence"* was coined in the 1950s, intending to describe the ability of machines to perform tasks at a human intelligence level. Today, the definition encompasses more nuanced meanings, especially when considering the level of human cognition. In this regard, there seem to be four categories: (1) automation; (2) machine learning using artificial neural networks; (3) deep learning; (4) and beyond.

Automation represents a low cognitive process that is repeatable, having well-defined sequences of actions that are pre-programmed into machine behaviour. The machine is a passive executor of what is being instructed to accomplish. Its ability to complete complex computations fast and without error is superior to humans. Automation can be applied on a large scale, with numerous examples from manufacturing production lines, to, more recently, interactions with customers, such as onboarding operations. It has the most concrete social impact, as it does take away jobs as we know them today. However, it also opens the opportunity for humans to do what they are better at than machines are: empathy, critical thinking, and creativity. The key to staying ahead of automation is, as Garry Kasparov puts it, *"human ambition."*

Machine learning using artificial neural networks requires a more sophisticated, yet still moderate level of cognition. The machine can mimic repeatable but personalized activities, while learning from each interaction, and utilizing increasing amounts of data. It reacts to events based on what was instructed to be accomplished. In other words, it can present a solution to a problem as posed, recommend tasks, or take simple actions. For example, it can automatically set up preferences at home, adjust ambient environment parameters based on these preferences, turn appliances on/off, or keep track of our grocery list. This stage has developed in leaps and bounds during the last decade or so, achieving results in recognition and even digitization of image, face, or speech. However, the machine still has difficulty perceiving at a level comparable to a human. Although we are still irritated by recommendations gone wrong or irrelevant comments coming from the chat box, we allow this type of artificial intelligence into our lives, without yet understanding its concrete positive and negative impacts.

The leap to deep learning is the phase that debuted only a few years ago. With big visions at the forefront, deep learning aims to build capacity for a machine to solve problems without being told how. Such machines mimic the brain, through layers of artificial neurons that connect with and send signals to each other in the network. Initial results are astounding. For example, the machine has been able to beat humans at Go, the complex ancient Chinese game, whose number of alternative positions surpasses the atoms in the universe. However, it seems we have yet to uncover what is happening inside these deep neural networks. Scientists are currently investigating adversarial examples, in which the difference between what the human and machine sees is extreme (e.g., turtle versus gun).

Beyond deep learning is yet an area for even bigger dreams in which, perhaps, machines will surpass the human brain capacity, being able to create symbol systems (e.g., language, money, time, religion, governance) and with that, structurally alter every aspect of the life as we know it.

It seems we are now somewhere during the development of the second category, machine learning, and in the early stages of the third one, deep learning.

We have been warned that *"Artificial Intelligence will best humans at everything by 2060."* With the many and contradicting opinions though, one could wonder, what will human capacity be in 2060? How will our brain functions evolve, and with that, where will our creativity, empathy, ambition, and critical thinking take us?

Do you wonder how to ignite futures for a regenerative society?

A growing and moving human population, as experienced in recent history, has expanding needs, wants, and desires. Such motivations have led to the creation of an amplifying artificial universe of things that is at odds with existing resources. The tension obstructs resource regeneration. How might we ignite futures that alleviate that tension?

It seems that the artificial societal constructs established in past centuries, able to harmonise society at other historical crossroads, have not been able to keep up with the society of 2018. Could we ignite regenerative futures by redesigning these artificial societal constructs?

A metaphor to imagine the complexity of natural and artificial constructs in society could be a tree. Imagine the roots of a tree as representing the natural constructs of society, comprised of cultural dynamics and their intertwinement with nature. The trunk of the tree would represent the artificial constructs of society: organization, governance, and civic engagement. The interactions amongst societal organization, governance, and engagement would proliferate as branches, each with a different length. The forms of expressions we desire in society might spring out in the leaves of a tree. They could include our aims for freedom of speech, aspirations for literacy, anchoring our lives in values such as trust, or daily life enjoyments such as healthy eating.

The methods of understanding for how we might achieve those forms of expression would be ingrained within the stem of the tree. The imaginary stem would require the wisdom of sketching the unthinkable coupled with the making of artificial things, including intelligence. A vibrant tree both lives and regenerates. A vibrant society assures daily life in the context of a regenerative paradigm.

The vision might look naïve to many. A regenerative society might seem yet another utopia. Businesses must respond to the realities of making it to the next quarter, diminishing their ability bandwidth to consider longer time horizons. Sciences are anchored in evidence-based and deterministic causal requirements, challenging imagined future worlds that lack traditional proofs.

The vision might resonate with the humanities field. Artists and designers provoke our imagination. Social scientists raise awareness. They are more likely to anchor their voices in the complexity of human nature and its surrounding environment. However, they still struggle to find a common view on basic concepts such as what "social" means.

The vision makes sense to many inter-disciplinarians. The struggle is in finding a language that resonates across disciplines. Each defines a similar concept in different ways. Historically, multiple disciplines come to the table, present their view, listen to other opinions, and then leave without much progress in a common understanding and commitment to igniting regenerative action. Finding a common language doesn't seem to work. Perhaps this is an indication that a common language does not matter?

Facilitating diverse dialogues that ignite action through societal engagement seems to register some progress though. Although timid, the discussions could gain vigour when supported by societal constructs fitted for 2018 and beyond. Could today's changemakers get inspired by earlier generations of visionaries who, at times when societal complexities were exacerbated, created innovative policies or treaties that broke down convoluted environments and drove society forward?

Monica Porteanu

Would A Post-Capitalist Economy Be One Which Catered For Values More Than Possessions?

1. Society, the economy, and the planet

2. Travelling along the scale of scarcity and abundance (and back?)

3. The Cycles of Life

4. Grow not stop. Which response to the wicked problem will we choose?

5. Morality First, Knowledge Second?

6. Economics lessons from wild nature

7. Can a storm in a coffee cup change the world?

8. Heroes on the edge

9. Social Entrepreneurs – Fashion or Future?

10. Will robots teach us to care?

11. Narratives Which Inspire Better Futures

12. Ticket to the Future

Society, the economy, and the planet

In the lead-up to the festive season, streets are dressed up in chic decorations, stores experiment with creative stands with sweets and gifts, and wherever we are, we can hardly escape from commercials, kindly offering to help us choose presents for our nearest and dearest. The hustle in the media and in the shops became an inseparable part of this special time and we can hardly imagine it to be otherwise. End of the year's shopping boom is good for us and good for businesses, right?

At the same time, a different announcement nearly got lost in this busy media clutter. The World Meteorological Organisation reported 2016 results which show the record increase in global carbon dioxide level in the atmosphere (403.3 ppm for those who like figures) - a rate not seen for millions of years. The increase is largely attributed to human activities, including the burning of fossil fuels. Those fuels keep our homes warm (or cool), make (most of) our cars move, enable the production of all the things that we need (and the ones that we don't really need), and help me write this post by powering my laptop with electricity.

Until now the price of most of these goods and services did not include full environmental costs and we only start considering this now, possibly too late and too slow. The Paris Agreement on Climate Change is the first attempt to address the issue on a big scale. With Syria recently having signed up the accord, all the countries in the world agreed to act collaboratively to limit the negative impact of human activities. The United States has become the only one leaving, as announced by Donald Trump earlier in 2017. Trump's reasoning is that the terms of the agreement are bad for America's economy (which is, by the way, the world's second-largest emitter of carbon). In other words, if the United States commits to the accord, they will not be able to produce as much stuff as they do now, as profitably as currently.

The reason for Trump's decision is in the short-term thinking and capitalistic values behind it. But he is not alone in prioritising the more tangible short-term outcomes over the more blurred future on the horizon. Generally, as recent research by the University of California suggests, human brains are "not wired for the future". However, as with everything, there are exceptions and in another part of the world, we find a different story.

While Trump is trying to protect the production of new goods, Sweden introduced a 50% reduction in tax on repairing goods. This is the government's attempt to rationalise new economic behaviour for people to revive their possessions, instead of buying new stuff; to create the new norms, as opposed to what developed countries are accustomed to. The initiative aims to cut carbon emissions from production, reduce waste and more generally, promote sustainable consumption. In other words, Sweden gives its citizens an additional, financial reason to take care of the planet. Sustainable values of responsible citizens are supported both by making this behaviour normal in society and by providing monetary rewards. And Swedes don't seem to expect any negative economic outcomes from the new law.

The difference between the responses of these two countries to the wicked problems we face is in how much weight the future has in the decisions we take today? The Brundtland Report in 1987 gave rise to the most influential definition of sustainable development. It states: "...development that meets the needs of the present without compromising the ability of future generations to meet their own needs". The difference between the Swedish and the American response is exactly in defining the needs of the present and in understanding the impact of today on the generations of the future.

While the governments of different countries may choose different actions in regard to these two components of sustainability, we are curious about whether we will see a more American or a more Swedish response from consumers in the future? We are not inviting you to re-gift your last year's present or to carry a Christmas tree home on a bicycle. The problem is much more complex than that and the solution involves all three parties: government, businesses and consumers.

What role will we choose to play? What is the relationship between our values, societal norms, economic conditions and our buying behaviour? When will we start including full environmental costs in the price of the goods and services and when will we be ready to pay for it? Will it direct our choices between alternative goods? Or not?

Travelling along the scale of scarcity and abundance (and back?)

It was a hot, late spring day from my childhood in Moscow of the early 1990s. My grandmother and I simmering in a long, slowly moving, queue in front of a grocery store. For a couple of months, the stalls have been nearly empty, with just very, very limited food available. In the pre-internet age, it made our "trips of hope" to the nearby stores a daily routine. That day we were lucky: they had cheese, hence such a hustle.

Towards lunch time the queue started moving faster, testing my excitement. When it was our turn, I noticed with surprise that the door was defended by a bulky store assistant in a uniform, acting like a gate-keeper. The gate-keeper, who happened to be equipped with a pen, left some sort of autograph on my grandma's hand, amplifying my confusion. Then we left. On the way home, my grandmother explained that the store was closing for a lunch break and the autograph was, in fact, our number in the queue, so that we could re-join it an hour later.

What happened after that has vanished from my recollection of that day. Although various forms of queues are still a common practice, the experience of being quite literally numbered in a queue to satisfy a most basic need left a more profound imprint in my memory than whether we actually had cheese on the table that day.

Today, in many countries consumer experience is opposite to that of post-Soviet Russia: the abundance of products makes brands hunt for consumers. Marketers spend billions of dollars on media budgets, packaging, new product development and the purchase of our data, trying to make us healthier, smarter, better people and simplifying the journey from our need to their product.

The trends of recent years indicate that additional variables have already started impacting consumer decision-making. Consumers increasingly see their purchases as a statement about their identity, portraying an image they want to be known for. This raises expectations from the brands to improve transparency, become greener and more efficient if they want to recruit more consumers to their team. Companies like Method, Lush and Everlane are already actively exploring the new area of purposeful marketing, while the agency enso.co is publishing a World Value Index which ranks brands not in terms of their business success but based on what they do for the world. Will this be enough to create a positive impact at scale? Or will other factors remain prevalent drivers of our purchases until something else will radically change our perception of responsibility as consumers?

While enso.co is rating brands, the Chinese government (although not necessarily driven by sustainability agenda) is rating its citizens. China is undertaking a massive project of implementing a social credit system. Once rolled-out in 2020, it will rank each and every citizen based on the individual's economic and social behaviour, as well as the scores of others in the person's network. Things like purchases in last week's shopping, frequent contacts circle or behaviour such as not showing up to a restaurant without cancelling your reservation – all this will count towards your personal score if you are a Chinese citizen in two years' time.

This reward and punishment system opens a big controversy. It is hard to say whether it will actually do more good or harm to society. No matter whether we would want to live a world like this or not, let's imagine that the mix of the two rating ideas from above is in place: a social credit system which rates us in regard to what we do for sustainability of the world. Each time we purchase a product from a particular place or brand, or buy a coffee in a plastic cup, our public image gets shaped and our personal rating is adjusted up and down on the scale.

And what if, in a possible future, when the scarcity of natural resources is fast approaching, and unsustainable behaviour is stigmatised in the society, our personal sustainability rating is used to allow or prohibit access to resources we need? What if this number, not written with ink on your hand, but publicly available in all databases mentioning your name, will again become our position in the line for limited resources? Will we then change our behaviour? And, most importantly, how can we change it now, so that we do not end up in such a world?

The Cycles of Life

Ouroboros – a snake eating its own tail. In many ancient cultures across the globe, this symbol represented the infinite cycle of renewal of life, a rebirth of the Earth, the continuous development of consciousness. We got used to the renewable nature of the world and learned how to benefit from it. Over centuries, humanity has been focussing on getting better, faster, more efficient – taking everything we do to the next level. In a search for better life, we tamed many types of energy, speed and even time, thanks to the advancements in health care. What is the driving force that makes us continuously strive for more, creating demand for overly saturated markets and often unnecessary exploitation of Earth?

Apparently, the answer may lay in Darwin's Evolution by Natural Selection. Canadian evolutionary psychologists ran multiple experiments which demonstrated the link between the natural selection modules that help species survive in the wild and our consumption habits. Survival module, sexual selection, kin selection and reciprocity – all these mechanisms from the jungle still exist in our casual lives and are covertly guiding our behaviour in grocery stores and shopping malls. They help us make the "safest" choices as dictated by the millions of years spent in a continuous fight for survival. Examples of this might be purchasing several flavours of the same type of food instead of one (to make sure we won't die in the event of it being poisonous), buying things that make us look more attractive (to be selected by a sexual partner with more promising genes), or acquiring possessions that help a desirable group identify us as a part of their tribe. Eventually, we often end up with an amount of stuff far beyond what we need.

If this behaviour has been in our genes for generations, does it mean that as consumers we will always be primarily guided by these instincts? Maslow addresses this in his "Theory of Human Motivation" where he links our motivations to the needs we have in a particular point of time or stage of life. But allegedly, Maslow himself admitted that another theory does a better job in explaining the psychology of human development. In contrast to his focus on an individual, Graves' theory of Spiral Dynamics explains the social and psychological development of a person and humanity in general.

This data-based approach to psychology charts the transformation in values and worldviews that humanity went through to the present, and the ones emerging. Initially, eight levels (later updated with additional one) represent different ways of how people think about things and respond to the world around them. They suggest that as the challenges we face change, so does our response to them, supported by the evolving consciousness. Like in a video game, upper levels, emerging in the context of new challenges, prompt different ways of thinking and worldviews that did not exist before.

No level is better than others and all of them coexist at any point in time. For simplicity, each level was assigned a colour. For this conversation, the most interesting is a shift between the two levels in the mid-upper part of the spiral: orange and green. Orange is about striving for success, competition, autonomy, working for abundance and reward. Think capitalism, Wall Street, show business or battles for "likes" in social media. Tired of the egocentric orange, following it, green is open to collaboration and inclusion. It values harmony, empathy and sensitivity and becomes environmentally conscious. Some estimates suggest that worldwide for every person with green attributes there are about three people with orange attributes.

We also see lots of pseudo-green happening in the orange world with some companies using sustainability and CSR messages more as marketing tools, rather than being truly guided by these values. What matters is that at the end of the day, together with the actions of those genuinely concerned about the future of the planet, this might be slowing down the speed of destruction in the age of Anthropocene.

The question remains though, which will happen quicker: will we collectively break-through to the next cycle of human consciousness or cross a biophysical threshold to a point of no return? How much of our own tail have we eaten already? And do we need a disaster – a problem of the next level of complexity – to activate our next cycle of consciousness?

Grow not stop. Which response to the wicked problem will we choose?

Grow not stop. Where shall we put the comma in this sentence? For a long time, growth has been the key focus of countries' GDPs, business plans and individual's bonus schemes. But is it really a good way to measure our progress towards a better life? What is a "good life" anyway? And what does our good life mean for its key enabler – the Earth?

A group of British scientists recently tried to answer some of these questions, namely: *is it possible for everyone to live a good life within our planet's limits?* They defined a good life very modestly – the satisfaction of basic needs – yet the result of their analysis of 150 countries is quite disheartening. Put on a map, the countries we know as well developed (Germany, Australia, Sweden, US, Japan) are clustered in the dangerous corner, having surpassed multiple biophysical boundaries. Moreover, if we were to try to equally distribute this modest standard of living for every person on the planet, we would need to use up to six times fewer resources than what is sustainable. Quite a sobering calculation, isn't it?

This study is not the first to address issues concerning our growth-oriented society. Back in 1987, the Brundtland Report called for changing the quality of growth. It stated: *"Sustainable development involves more than growth. It requires a change in the content of growth, to make it less material and energy-intensive, and more equitable in its impact."* The report alerted that growth combined with acute inequality can be worse for a country's development than the lack of growth. Currently, in 2018, we are obviously a long way from either reducing inequality or growing sustainably.

A contemporary economist, Kate Raworth addresses the same growth-related issues and warns about the obsolescence of the economic theory taught in schools and universities. In her book "Doughnut Economics" she urges us to shift the focus from the growth in GDP towards creating a more just society instead. To treat natural resources as an integral part of economics, not some loosely related externality. Although her book was shortlisted by the Financial Times as one of the best business books of 2017, Ms. Raworth points to the challenges of getting outdated academic views replaced by a more accurate and holistic understanding of economics. In an attempt to make this change happen, Ms Raworth invites us to start a guerrilla campaign to fight against the invalid economic dogmas in a non-traditional way.

At the same time, students in Oregon, US have chosen to act even more radically to ensure their voices are heard. They took the federal government to court for *"profoundly damaging our home planet by subsidizing fossil-fuel production which violated [the government's] public-trust responsibility and threatens the plaintiffs' fundamental constitutional rights to life and liberty"*. This accusation probably goes beyond any other environmental case so far. The outcome of this case is still pending, but other similar cases initiated by plaintiffs between 10 and 20 years old may start to see some success around the world.

What is an appropriate response when the traditional structures are so imperfect? When teens who compete to study in the best universities, hoping to get the knowledge they need to change the world, graduate from their courses to be disappointed by the obsolete theory they were taught. When representatives we elect to act on our behalf go astray, blinded by the short-term goals linked to their terms of power. Is it a revolt like the one in 2014 organised by economics students in 30 countries against a curriculum disconnected from reality? Is it a guerrilla campaign to stealthily re-draw diagrams in university books like Kate Raworth proposes? Do we have to go as far as taking to court the very government we elected, like the boys and girls from iMatter and other environmental groups do? What actions should citizens take to make sure that the voices of future generations are heard at the tables where big decisions are made?

Something that each of us could do is at least to make sure that our own children get a systemic, big picture view of the world, as opposed to narrow opinions dictated by short-term capitalistic values. Knowing what the choice *actually* means of a comma's position in the "grow not stop" sentence might become a much more important knowledge in our kids' life than many other things in their curriculum. The question remains though – is it enough?

Morality First, Knowledge Second?

If you have ever travelled around Vietnam, you might have noticed at the main entrance of some schools the motto, previously ubiquitous in the communist era: *"Tien hoc le, hau hoc van"*. The direct meaning refers to the importance to learn proper manners in human relations first, and only then start learning other things that you would normally learn at school. Loosely it can be translated as *"morality comes before knowledge"*. In the past, it has served as a good call for millions of Vietnamese students and really, would not hurt anyone to be reminded of it. We are wondering if this prioritisation would still be applicable to our world of rapidly growing technologies?

The past couple of months offered us some food for thought on the evolution of business ethics in the light of technological progress.

- Facebook makes money from selling our data, which it gets in exchange for letting us share this very data free of charge – is it a fair deal? While regulators are only attempting to catch up with technicalities of this business model, Facebook continues benefiting from this knowledge gap.

- The first pedestrian died from an autonomous car approved by Uber for public roads, even with a vehicle operator behind the steering wheel. Was it human complacency with an autonomous vehicle offering a relaxing ride? Did the launch of the system happen too early, rushed by the appetite for quicker return on investments? Or was it the lack of maturity in this field that prevented good judgement on whether the system is ready for operation?

What previously was good or bad as black and white, has now shifted into a grey area.

While in these cases Facebook users and Uber testing the driverless technology might be victims of ignorance and lack of caution, some other innovations make us concerned about the way the ethics of *consumers* might evolve in the future in our market society. Augmented reality and cruel video games; robots and the sex industry; more generally, robots as household servants (or slaves?). One can say that whatever people choose to do in their free time is their business, but wouldn't it be naive to assume that the change in our own morality will have no implication for society?

A further twist to these already ambiguous scenarios came out of the study on human-robot interaction conducted by researchers from MIT and Stanford. Their experiments have shown that when people work with autonomous robots and errors occur, humans tend to blame the robots rather than themselves. Interestingly, when success occurs, we humans take the credit more frequently than giving it to the machine. In other words, our habit to shift responsibility for mistakes from ourselves to other people remains unchanged when we get to deal with autonomous tech-friends instead of our familiar colleagues.

This poses further questions on what implications this might have for ethics in a high-tech post-capitalistic world. Who will take responsibility for decisions made by a board which consists of both humans and AI? One of the first non-human board directors – VITAL – already gets to vote in board meetings together with five human directors in a venture capital firm in Hong Kong. While VITAL only takes decisions on investments, where its skills in scanning large volumes of data come in particularly handy, we can only imagine how this might play out with advancements in deep learning. Will we still be sure that the machine is acting in the company's interests? And if reality shows the opposite, who is to blame?

How will ethical decision-making evolve in the future? Will it be something a majority demands? Something the powerful agree on? Or something that AI would recommend as the least harmful option? What is clear is that it is becoming increasingly dependent upon how much we know about technology and its implications for society. Knowledge starts to inform morality and we should challenge ourselves to stay up to speed to make sure we take decisions that meet our moral standards.

Economics lessons from wild nature

If we try to apply Darwin's theory of evolution to economic systems, would we conclude that capitalism "better suits to the environment" (better suits us) than communism? After all, most of ex-communist countries shifted to capitalism and the majority of the few remaining are now transitioning to free market economies. Have we naturally selected the better way? Apparently, only half of us would agree. According to a recent online survey of twenty thousand people in 28 countries run by the research company Ipsos, half of respondents around the globe think that now, in the

21st century, "socialist ideals are of great value for societal progress".

What exactly ideals are these? Here are some stats:

- 9 in 10 believe that education should be free, and that free healthcare is a human right
- 7 in 10 think that everyone should have the right to an unconditional basic income (UBI).
- Interestingly, about the same number (7 in 10) also agree that it is right for people who are talented to earn more than those who are less gifted, and that free market competition brings out the best in people.

It seems that although the benefits of free markets in fostering progress are valued, when it comes to the essential aspects of life – health, welfare, education – many of us are craving for a more egalitarian system; the one alleviating the polarizing inequality that capitalism has created.

With so many innovations fostering humanity's progress being inspired by nature, we are curious: what examples of democratic distribution of resources exist in the wild world? One study particularly attracted our attention. A Belgian-French group of scientists studied self-organised collective decision-making by animals when it comes to choosing between alternative resources.

They ran an experiment where 50 cockroaches *(Blattella germanica)* were presented with three shelters, each with a capacity to hold 40 individuals. For cockroaches, who prefer darkness to light, such a shelter is a resource, and they quickly filled them in. But instead of doing this in a chaotic manner, the cockroaches split into two equal groups of 25 occupying two shelters and leaving the third one empty. While in a scenario with larger shelters – each big enough for the whole group – only one of the shelters got occupied. The researchers were astonished by how cockroaches maximise the benefit of limited resources, trading off being together and access to shelter resources and finding a balance between collaboration and competition. "Without elaborate communication, global information, and explicit comparison of available opportunities, [...] the collective decision emerges from the interactions between equal individuals, initially possessing little information about their environment. It is remarkable, then, that these rules should produce a *collective* pattern that maximizes *individual* fitness."

Economic democracy observed in behaviour of cockroaches presents some of the features where capitalism and representative democracy did not quite succeed: egalitarian distribution of resource and decision-making benefiting all (or at least the majority of) individuals. It might seem too simplistic to directly compare the economic problems faced by *Blattella germanica* and those of *Homo sapiens*. But if we think of some emerging movements – collaborative mobile democracy, participatory budgeting, commons-based economic governance – are they not technologically empowered forms of truly collective decision-making, replicating those observed in nature? With new technologies making us more interconnected, we now have a unique opportunity to access the knowledge and opinions of all interested citizens and reshape the way we, as a society, take decisions and distribute value.

Following nature's principle of evolution, only a better system, distributive by design and maximising fitness of more individuals, will be able to replace capitalism by making it obsolete. Mother nature offers us many lessons, and the lesson of balancing collaboration and competition has been one of the hardest to comprehend. It requires both individual engagement and strong leadership ability to connect knowledge and talents from the community and to facilitate the best ideas evolving in something new.

As American sociologist Erik Olin Wright suggests, we cannot smash or escape capitalism, but we can tame or erode it. By slowly introducing new elements, inspired by nature and enabled by technology, we might start shifting the focus from maximising financial value and growth to real value creation and more equality. And then who knows... maybe one day this will make capitalism in its classical form obsolete.

Can a storm in a coffee cup change the world?

Previously, we proposed the idea that only a better system, distributive by design, will be able to replace capitalism by making it obsolete. Are there any models that could address existing market failures? Can social entrepreneurship, combining the best of business and charity, play this role?

Social entrepreneurship has taken off in recent years. According to the Social Business Initiative of the European Commission, one in four start-ups in Europe is what we could call social enterprises. One in three starter-uppers-to-be wants to become a social entrepreneur. Where did this boom come from? New technologies certainly offer new opportunities, while the emerging shift in values is another key reason. For today's employees – especially millennials, who now make up more than half of the workforce – purpose at work has become more important than ever. Yet it is not always easy to find in the corporate world.

In Deloitte's survey of 10,455 millennials across 36 countries, nearly two-thirds agreed that corporations "have no ambition beyond wanting to make money." Is this why People & Culture consultants advise organisations to improve staff engagement by creating a *"sense of purpose"*? The question is though: do employers get anything in return, but a *sense* of engaged workforce? Fewer and fewer university graduates are buying into a post-engineered pro-social purpose of a business, originally designed purely to maximise the value of its owners. Disillusioned by the lack of well-paid purposeful roles in the public and not-for-profit sectors, more and more millennials choose to set up their own business the way they feel would be right.

Social entrepreneurs use their passion, creative talent and new technologies to address the wicked problems which most businesses are not interested to solve, and traditional public, voluntary or community mechanisms do not succeed in. This approach is also interesting in that it invites customers to become a part of the solution, potentially shifting their values as well.

Erick Jantsch in his theory of social planning suggests that when a new behavior, introduced by a group of innovators, becomes normative in a society, the values are more likely to change, too. Take a takeaway coffee cup. Some ten years ago, in Moscow, for me as a fresh graduate, getting a coffee in a single-use take-away cup was a symbol of freedom. It was a metaphor for independence of adulthood. An escape from the iron-curtained Soviet times. Coolness and confidence at the same time. What happened to the symbol after the last sip of coffee did not bother me whatsoever. Now in Melbourne, world famous for its coffee culture, I feel embarrassed to ask for a coffee in a single-use cup, of which only the lid can be recycled. It does not support the values I have developed. It does not fit my brand. With reusable cups – social innovation introduced by what you can probably call social entrepreneurs – now conquering the world, it feels irresponsible to stick to the unsustainable option.

When this initial behavioral shift happens, even if only among early adopters, behavior that used to be normative is challenged and becomes up for grabs for social change. Businesses catch up by offering a discount for customers who come with their reusable cup. If governments introduce new legislation at this point in the change process, it won't be seen ridiculous anymore (well, perhaps only by plastic ware manufacturers), and the shift in values will continue spreading. Fundamental changes happen when people change their minds, not when policy dictates them. By the time my kids get into drinking coffee, I am hopeful that non-recyclable cups will only be found in museums.

In a similar way, can social entrepreneurship establish new business behaviour which, over time, will challenge the current capitalistic values? Will its pressure on the traditional economic system be strong enough to influence legislation and create tangible disruption to the businesses with "no ambition beyond money"? Does it have the potential to become the "post-capitalism thing"? And what is needed for this to happen?

Heroes on the edge

Social entrepreneurship is winning more and more hearts and minds. It is showing the potential to disrupt traditional business models. For now, it is still quite niche and will need to come a long way to be seriously considered as an evolution of capitalism. The time required for the sector to mature and the broader ecosystem to introduce mechanisms for collaboration is one reason. Yet the main cause is probably that it is just bloody hard to be a social entrepreneur.

Not only you face all the issues that most start-ups are too familiar with – unstable cash flow, scalability, securing high product quality with limited resources – there is also an additional level of complexity: delivering on the promise to give back to the community. To make things harder, it is not enough just to be doing good – you are expected to demonstrate that your approach is working. With social impact in the heart of the business proposition, it is essential to be radically transparent about profit and how it gets distributed. For a social enterprise, earning customers' trust is more critical than almost for anyone else: no customer wants to find out that the dollars they spent to support a social cause have sponsored someone's luxurious vacation. And trust takes time.

On top of the challenges of these early days when social entrepreneurship is toddling its way into the big economic system, we would argue that some of the obstacles are created by the entrepreneurs themselves. The very unconformity which drives social entrepreneurs to start their own business in the first place might be doing them a disservice at a later stage. Surveys suggest that after the paramount motivation to make the difference, the key motives driving these starter-uppers are the need for acknowledgment and heroism. Combined with a strong attachment to a specific social issue, this might make collaboration with other entrepreneurs more difficult. Opportunities to make more impact with joint forces are being missed. This leads to the high fragmentation of the social entrepreneurship ecosystem which slows down the development of the sector.

Previously, we touched on the lessons that business can adopt from nature. Is there a recipe from the wild world which would help social entrepreneurs? Potentially, yes – the phenomenon called *the edge effect*. In ecology, the edge effect happens at the boundary where two ecosystems, such as forest and savannah, meet. This is the place where many forms of life are born. By drawing on the distinct features of the two different habitats, edge effect creates the environment for unprecedented biodiversity. A lot has been said about the importance of diversity for innovation, and social innovation is not different.

Stepping out of the zone where you have full control, letting the certainty go and trusting emergence might not be easy. This is the time and space when one might get uncomfortable with the ambiguity of how the future might unfold. This space is called liminal space – the threshold where the solutions from the past are not effective anymore and the new solutions are only shaping. Despite the discomfort, with a little luck and trust this space might uncover completely new answers to an old problem – it can show the way to innovation.

To part with one's personal ambitions in order to amplify social impact might be hard. But if we truly want to make a sustainable change, we need to move from *ego-* to *eco-*system, as Otto Scharmer puts it. We live in the time when we need not heroes but leaders. Leaders, who sense how to jump on an opportunity, able to think in systems, connect the dots and connect with people, drawing on the collective talent.

In the age of connected devices, our ability to collaborate and to come up with creative solutions is one of the key traits differentiating us from machines; it needs to be cherished. We need to shift from problem-solution matching to the recognition that many of today's issues don't have a known solution. Trusting collective co-creation process can get us closer to finding what works. By going beyond the edge for more collaboration, social entrepreneurs could accelerate social innovations. This could help the whole sector more quickly to become a more serious alternative to traditional business.

Finding yourself at the edge might feel uncomfortable, but what if a step forward would give us wings?

Social Entrepreneurs – Fashion or Future?

Previously we have discussed the potential of social entrepreneurship to make a shift in social values and to address wicked problems through social innovation. What changes in public and private sectors are needed for social entrepreneurship to become future-proof in the capitalistic world?

Government is starting to play an enabling role in the development of the sector. Initiatives like social enterprise strategies, social procurement or social impact investment start to reshape institutional and cultural frameworks of the past. Procuring services from a social enterprise or from a traditional vendor might make no difference in terms of the services received. But it does make a difference for people from disadvantaged groups who get the job or for those from vulnerable groups who benefit from the redistributed profit. Yet, a significant maturity of legislation is still required to better define this sector and to help other players understand what a social enterprise is and what it is not.

Another legislative change needed is about the behaviour that gets incentivised. What if governments would support businesses which are driven not by the desire to maximise profit, but which put community first? This step might seem counterintuitive in the market economy, but it turns out that a government operating based on the principles of commons already exists.

Municipalists, such as Barcelona en Comú – a new movement, independent from political parties – challenge the current understanding of democracy by putting the common goals of city residents in the heart of their policy-making. Despite conservative politicians initially criticising them for being naive, lacking understanding where city money comes from and even tagging them "the democratic mistake", en Comú proved they were fit to serve the community in just a couple of years.

By focusing on the needs of the most vulnerable population, they:

- do business only with hotels that agree to pay a living wage
- create new affordable housing, many of which were previously vacant bank-owned units
- looking at extending store opening hours to address the economy of care – mostly female part of the population whose primary labour is caring for others
- and even launched a publicly held energy company.

According to the Mayor Ada Colau, they are "prioritising people and common objectives above any other vested interest and any other type of power". This would not turn any enterprise in a social enterprise, but is it a good enough shake-up for businesses to realise that the rules of the game are changing?

And what about businesses? Here as well we see emerging partnerships between corporates and social entrepreneurs. IKEA, for example, employs local artisans in vulnerable communities around the world. Through limited edition collections handcrafted by women from these communities, the company attempts to tackle social challenges: alleviate poverty, empower women and integrate refugees into a new to them society. They call it "business for good, for everyone". PR or an active social agenda? It does not matter. Remember Erick Jantsch's theory of social change? Once this initial change in behaviour, introduced by innovators, becomes a norm, a change in social values will follow.

And the process has started already. Australia's Good Company has announced its annual rating of Top 40 Best Workplaces to Give Back. Corporates compete to get on the list by providing pro bono work, sponsorship or volunteering. Is this a natural trajectory of evolution – from maximising shareholders value (and sometimes actively doing harm) to the understanding that this approach is not sustainable? Can we reach the other side of the scale, where maximising the value for the community will be essential to remain competitive? While social entrepreneurs are learning from corporations how to do business, can corporations learn from social entrepreneurs how to make business good-for-all?

Will robots teach us to care?

The last couple of months have been particularly loud with all things about women's rights. From the freedom to change a T-shirt on a tennis court to gender equality at C-level roles – the world seems to be going through some sort of "Equality Checklist" in all possible aspects of life. This made me curious: if one day we achieve the sort of gender equality we are seeking, what would the world look like? How would this play out with changes in other areas of life? And why are we trying to create this future in the first place?

These days many corporate and public bodies are trying to close gender equality gaps at every level of their organisation. At the same time, trend analyses indicate that ubiquitous robotisation will replace many of skilled labour jobs and free up people for work... in the care sector. These jobs require the ability to connect emotionally, build relationships and empathise – the qualities robots don't have. According to the International Labour Organisation, two-thirds of these jobs are occupied by women; and traditionally they haven't been valued much. There is hope that being less replaceable by machines, this type of work will become more valued and more attractive in the future.

Indeed, one of the perverse attributes of capitalistic society is that we value and incentivise work which is directly linked to visible outcomes, such as profit, growth or innovation. It gets all the credit. While its enabler – caring work, a lot of which is unrecognised and unpaid, such as looking after kids, elderly or people with disabilities – remains in the shadow. With our habit to define each other by what we do, somehow work as a full-time mum or carer has become a negligible (not to mention unprofitable) occupation. But can we be successful in business when our family is not cared for? Or, as futurist Alvin Toffler used to ask: "How productive would your workforce be if it hadn't been toilet trained"?

Due to the current perception of care work as a second-rate occupation and related low pay, we already don't have enough care workers to look after those in need. Although there is no certainty whether these jobs will be better paid for in the future, it's quite likely that robotisation will push more people to become a part of the economy of care, even if only as a way to maintain social bonds. At the end of the day, being useful for somebody is a part of human nature; and getting paid for it is a by far better alternative to the unemployment bench. This will, in turn, lead to a more even gender distribution in this job segment, further contributing to it being valued more.

Had traditional female roles as carer received a proper role in the economy, would we see this push for gender equality in the business world? Would more people be choosing carer roles, knowing that they will receive a decent pay and recognition? Equality is not about blindly erasing differences between men and women. Nether it is only about providing equal opportunities at the top of the career ladder. What is missing is the recognition of the importance of the carer work which enables our progress as a society and re-writing economic models to make it a true part of the economy. It requires a cultural change and the revision of our values. By reshaping the future of work, robotisation is expected to be a driving force for this shift. But do we have to wait for it to start caring for carers?

Narratives Which Inspire Better Futures

The address by New Zealand's Prime Minister Jacinda Ardern at 2018 UN Assembly caused an eruption of applause. She devoted a lot of her speech to a call-for-action on climate change: "Our action in the wake of this global challenge remains optional, but the impact of inaction does not." This is a very good point, indeed. This type of challenge requires strong political leadership across the globe with a clear, long-sighted shared vision. And yet, despite the destructive impact of human activities being obvious by now, we still are not doing enough to change the course. Why?

For Jean Tirole, the winner of the Nobel prize in Economics, this is a no-brainer. "It is the result of two factors" – Tirole says – "selfishness with regard to future generations and the free rider problem. In other words, the benefits of reducing climate change remain global and distant in time, while the costs of that reduction are local and immediate." Although there are attempts to internalise the negative externalities, for example, by means of carbon tax, they are far from perfect. For example, carbon leakage – moving contaminating production from a country with stricter environmental regulation to a country where it's cheaper to pollute – makes it clear that only a truly global solution could slow down climate change.

It is hard to motivate yourself to solve a problem which you don't see at this point in time in your immediate environment. Moreover, as studies show, our brains are biased towards more positive images of future and can even influence our perception of facts. Neither are helpful political systems based on short-term election cycles. They often make politicians prioritise the immediate outcomes promised to their electorate over the long-term improvements, the benefits of which might not be even seen by the current voting generation. But this is not the case everywhere.

For starters, China, allegedly, is halfway through its 100-year strategy. The strategy consists of nine steps, based on lessons from history, which are supposed to make China the world's leading superpower by 2050. Another example of long-term planning comes from indigenous people of North America. In Mohawk nation, historically based in present-day New York area, the chief is appointed by the clan mother for life. As part of his role, he should be making decisions based on the interests of the community "seven generations from now". Should the chief not be acting in the best interests of people, after three warnings the title can be taken away from him.

What elements of this long-term thinking can Western capitalistic societies adopt to represent the voices of yet-to-be-born generation in decisions we take today? Back to New Zealand which also seems to be inspired by its local communities. Learning from Maori's concept of guardianship – the idea that we have a duty of care for the environment that we pass on to future generations – New Zealand is aiming to become *the best place in the world to be a child*. This encompasses not only young Kiwis' childhood experience but also the prospects for their future, the country, and the environment today's generation hands over to them.

While other countries are working on policies and strategies aiming for similar outcomes, the way New Zealand communicates it seems to be different. It unites various strategies under one inspiring goal which reveals a deeper meaning and images of the future behind the dry targets. Supported by strong engagement, it might become a powerful strategic narrative. It has an exciting potential to mobilise people's agency towards achieving a goal they can relate to.

Businesses have already started adopting narratives for strategic decision-making. To mature further, these narratives need to incorporate systemic thinking. A switch from pitching benefits of individual initiatives towards a better understanding of how pulling one trigger can influence another area could get us one step closer towards understanding how our actions impact our children's future.

In isolation, the narratives won't do the job. We need a united global action, internalisation of externalities and more systemic approach. This will only happen when all key parties will take a conscious decision to take these steps. But what a good narrative can do is to make a shift in thinking and inspire these actions that our future kids so desperately need.

Ticket to the Future

People introduced tickets as a mechanism to control access to limited goods and services. We are surrounded by tickets. A ticket on a plane reserves us a seat in a machine which will take us to new horizons. A visa allows us to stay in a place that is usually attractive enough to create an artificial contest for the right to be there. A membership provides you with services not available to others. You invest – you get access to an opportunity. If we are in a lucky position, we can choose the ticket and the destination. If we overlay this concept with the idea of a variety of possible futures awaiting us ahead, a ticket to which future do we want to get?

We have discussed this by looking at potential pathways for the post-capitalist economy. We were especially keen to know whether the universal moral values or the capitalistic cult for possessions will guide our future. The search for the answer took us to different corners of the planet where people's responses to the side-effects of capitalism are sparking hope that we might be heading towards a better future.

We saw young entrepreneurs jumping off the big and clumsy steam train of global corporations (successful if measured by their share price), because these people could not agree with the direction that they were heading towards. In the smog from ever increasing unsustainable production, they could not see the purpose to align with. We applauded to the municipalists movement in Barcelona, who understood that improved equality and long-term sustainability will make citizens happier than infinite growth benefiting a few. Not only they challenged the current understanding of democracy, but could demonstrate already in the first couple of years that their approach is working. We even joined a hearing in a US courtroom, where boys and girls from iMatter, already at a young age have become disillusioned with their government's ability to protect their needs and those of future generations. They refused to accept tickets to the future valid only till the end of the government's election term.

These steps towards the increased consciousness plant seeds of hope that the next iteration of economic system will be more sustainable and just. And yet, the embodiment of this hope to a greater extent depends on the choices that powerful global businesses will make. Many quoted this year's annual letter from the CEO of BlackRock – one of the most influential global investment firms. It stated that following new expectations from customers and community, they are now evaluating companies based on their response to "broader societal challenges" and whether they "serve a social purpose." The New York Times called the letter "a watershed moment on Wall Street" raising "questions about the very nature of capitalism".

The question remains though: what is driving the companies to make this shift? Does it happen out of fear to lose customer trust or investors' support, with profit remaining the underlying motive? If so, how significant can this social impact be? Does it become just another marketing tool for the same old endgame: more sales, more growth, more money?

Even then – we could hope – this shift could take us a little closer towards a more positive version of the future. Remember the coffee-cup example from our previous posts? Initially driven by a bunch of innovators, reusable coffee cups are now conquering the world, helping it to become a tiny bit more sustainable. Similarly, the new generation of businessmen growing up in the environment where creating positive social impact is becoming a norm might nurture values quite different to those ruling the capitalistic economy. In the face of increasingly challenging global issues, these values will help them to genuinely engage in revisiting unsustainable business models.

To what type of future humanity is heading depends on the tickets that each of us will choose. These tickets are a combination of choices that we make every day.

These are our "investments", each associated with a specific type of future. Can I give an example? Here you go.

We started this series just after last Christmas and as we finish it, the new Christmas season is approaching. If you are wondering what choices you could still make this year to contribute to a "good future destination" ticket, think of your Christmas presents. Consider not buying new stuff. Give your loved ones experiences. Give surprise visits to people you haven't seen for a long time. Give them your time and take them for a walk in a forest. Give them a ticket to joyful moments of life – they will never end up in landfill.

Polina Silakova

BIOGRAPHIES

Adam Cowart

Adam Cowart is a strategic foresight professional and playwright. He holds a creative writing B.F.A. and M.F.A. from the University of British Columbia, a M.B.A. from Simon Fraser University, and a M.Sc. in Foresight from University of Houston. He is also a six sigma blackbelt and a proud alum of the Stanford d.School's *Design Thinking Bootcamp* and Harvard's *Reimagining Strategy* executive education program.

His recently produced plays include *Entanglement* which premiered at the 2017 Impact Festival and *Definition of Time* at Vancouver's legendary Cultch theatre in 2014. Selected publications include co-authoring "Setting up a Horizon Scanning System: A U.S. Forestry Agency Example" in the World Futures Review: Vol 10, Issue 2, and "The Futurist's Menagerie" and "Pity the 1%" in Scenario magazine.

He is an Adjunct Professor in the University of Houston Foresight department and a Senior Project Manager for Loblaw Companies Limited. He is a member of the Professional Association of Futurists where he was named an Emerging Fellow in 2018, and a member of the Playwright's Guild of Canada. His research interests include mapping and design interventions of complex narrative ecosystems, and the influence of hyperstitional disruption on innovation and strategy formation.

E-mail: adam_cowart@hotmail.com

Craig Perry

Craig is an American futurist specializing in the international relations and global security sectors. After completing a degree in History at Brown University, he embarked on a long career as a U.S. Air Force officer, including assignments in Iraq, Korea, Germany, and Russia, where he served as an Olmsted Scholar at St. Petersburg State University.

Craig discovered strategic foresight while stationed in San Antonio, Texas, at the Joint Information Operations Warfare Center, where he led a team charged with analyzing the future of the information environment. He soon encountered a variety of government and military organizations engaged in similar foresight activities, and resolved to explore this field further at the University of Houston upon his retirement from the military. He received a master's degree from the Houston Foresight program in 2017. Craig now lives and works in the United Kingdom.

E-mail: *perryfutures@outlook.com*

Monica Porteanu

Monica Porteanu is a Ph.D. candidate in Design, Technology, and Society Informatics at the University of Illinois at Urbana-Champaign, advised by Professor Kevin Hamilton, New Media, and Dean, Fine and Applied Arts. Her research focuses on decision making for a regenerative society, aiming to apply data science and interactive design futures to navigate from data to impact. She hopes to shape engagements that inspire and drive progress and positive change for individual and collective members of society.

She holds a Master of Design in Strategic Foresight and Innovation from the Ontario College of Art and Design, an MBA from Cornell, and a BMath from Romania.

Monica is an Emerging Professional Futurist Fellow with the Association of Professional Futurists, a Fellow of the British Royal Society for the encouragement of Arts,

Manufactures and Commerce, a Canadian Certified Management Consultant, and a strategy consultant.

E-mail: mporteanu@ymail.com

Polina Silakova

Polina is a researcher, strategist and a creative storyteller, passionate about sustainable futures. For more than a decade she has been driving transformations in brands, operations, and corporate strategy. Her clients include such renown global brands as Nestle, Colgate-Palmolive, Bayer, Danone, SCA, Ferrero and many others. Following her passion for improving people's everyday lives, she delivered improvements in local and state government in Australia.

She uses her knowledge and skills in business and strategic foresight to analyse the dynamics in different domains, facilitate collaboration, help people create preferable futures and develop strategies for a sustainable change.

When not working on solving wicked problems, Polina can be found in a dance or yoga class or writing her next blog post. She is always on a search for opportunities to add value as a volunteer or mentor and to connect with thought-leaders around the world.

E-mail: polina.silakova@gmail.com

Stephen Aguilar-Millan

Stephen is the Director of Research of the European Futures Observatory, a Foresight Research Institute based in the UK, where he manages the research team.

The Observatory specialises in providing insights into how the world might be in the second half of this century. Stephen's specialisation within the team is directed towards the economy and the financial system, and how this may impinge upon future geo-politics. Stephen specialises in economic and financial wargaming, of which he has over 25 years of experience.

He holds a number of advisory positions with a number of public bodies around the world, and he advises a number of private sector firms on these matters.

E-mail: stephena@eufo.org

The Association of Professional Futurists

The Association of Professional Futurists is a global community of futurists, dedicated to promoting professional excellence and demonstrating the value of strategic foresight and futures studies for their clients and/ or employers. Futurists work in global corporations, small businesses, consultancies, education, non-profits, and government. Founded in 2002, the APF now includes more than 400 members from 40 countries.

The APF sets the standard of excellence for foresight professionals. Members include futurists from businesses, governments, non-profits, consulting futurists, educators, and students in future studies.

Our members meet regularly and host active online discussions among practitioners. We also provide professional development programs and recognition for excellence in futures works. We offer to both our members and the public our rich body of ideas and information about the future. Please see our Blog, by our members and emerging fellows.

We invite you to browse our web site and to engage our community. Here you will discover more about what we do and the members we represent.

www.apf.org